DIARY OF A DISCIPLE

LUKE'S STORY HOLIDAY CLUB

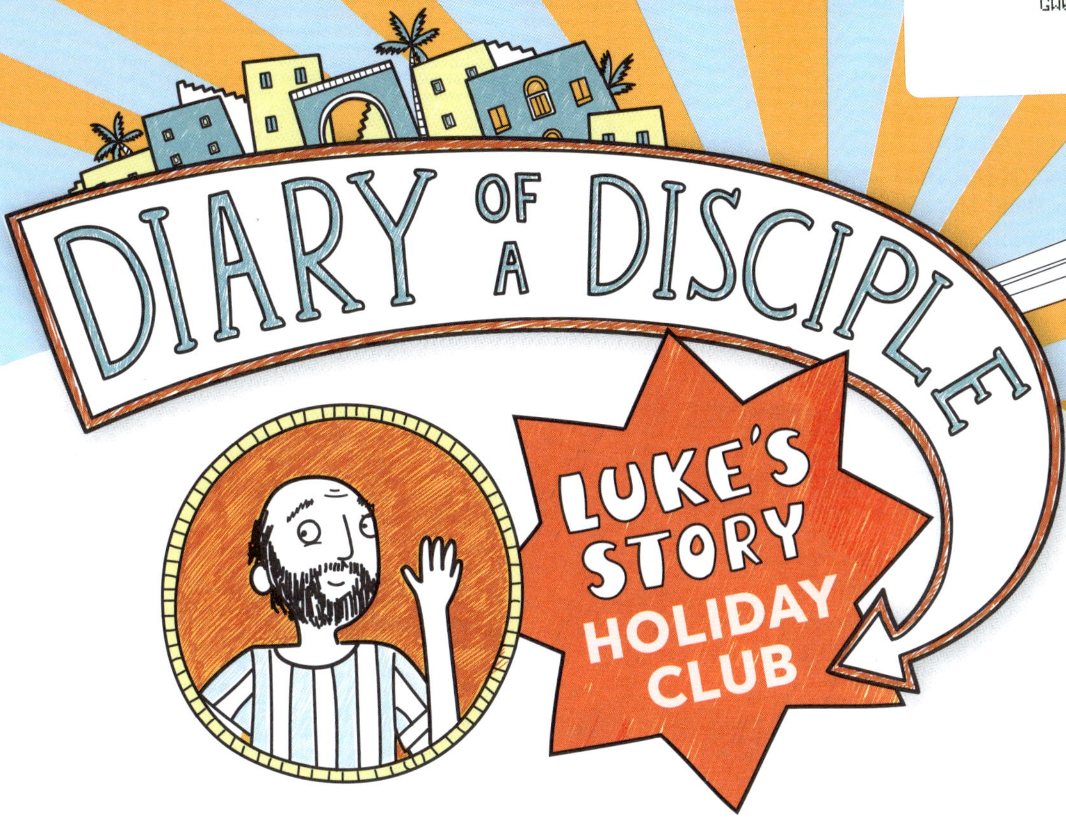

A three- to five-day holiday club based on **Luke's Gospel** from Scripture Union for 5- to 11-year-olds

© Scripture Union 2021

First published 2021

ISBN 978 1 78506 827 0

Scripture Union
Trinity House, Opal Court, Opal Drive, Fox Milne, Milton Keynes MK15 0DF
Email: info@scriptureunion.org.uk
Website: www.scriptureunion.org.uk

All rights reserved. No part of this publication may be reproduced, stored in a retrieval system, or transmitted in any form or by any means, electronic, mechanical, photocopying, recording or otherwise, without the prior permission of Scripture Union.

Scripture quotations are from the Contemporary English Version published by HarperCollins*Publishers* © 1991, 1992, 1995 American Bible Society

British Library Cataloguing-in-Publication Data

A catalogue record of this book is available from the British Library.

Printed in India by Nutech Print Services

Cover and internal design: kwgraphicdesign

Cover image and illustrations: Emma Randall

Writers: Sam Fowler, Helen Franklin, Steve Hutchinson, Margaret Lilley, Jenni Whymark, Gemma Willis

Scripture Union is an international Christian charity working with churches in more than 130 countries.

Thank you for purchasing this book. Any profits from this book support SU in England and Wales to bring the good news of Jesus Christ to children, young people and families and to enable them to meet God through the Bible and prayer.

Find out more about our work and how you can get involved at:
- www.scriptureunion.org.uk (England and Wales)
- www.suscotland.org.uk (Scotland)
- www.suni.co.uk (Northern Ireland)
- www.scriptureunion.org (USA)
- www.su.org.au (Australia)

CONTENTS

THE BASICS

Understanding the basics — 6
A new model — 6
A different approach — 7
Explore Together — 9

Overview and Bible programme — 11
Who do you say I am? — 11
Bible Day by Day — 11

Programme — 13
Programme elements — 13
Programme timetable — 14
Every Day items — 15

Team roles — 16
Core roles — 16
Other roles — 17

Small groups — 18
Leading good small groups and developing relationships — 18

Preparing your venue — 20
Registration and collection area — 20
Upfront area — 20
Daily decorations for the upfront area and venue — 21
Small group areas — 21
Explore Zones — 22

Adapting your club — 23
Children with additional needs — 23
Children from a 5% background — 23
Children from other faiths — 24
A note on registration and collection — 25

Additional resources — 26
Additional days — 26
Booklets for children — 26
Animations and audio stories — 27
Drama scripts — 27
Publicity — 27
Other downloadable resources — 27
Legal requirements and safeguarding — 27

Follow-on — 28
What next? — 28

DIARY DAYS

Day 1
Who is Jesus? — 30

Day 2
What did Jesus do and say? — 39

Day 3
What happened to Jesus? — 48

FOLLOW-ON
Faith journeys — 60

THE BASICS

UNDERSTANDING THE BASICS

Welcome to this *Diary of a Disciple: Luke's Story* holiday club! We're so pleased you've chosen to share the good news of Jesus with the children and young people in your community. This holiday club makes use of the book *Diary of a Disciple: Luke's Story*, which has proved really popular with children and extremely helpful in encouraging them in reading about the life of Jesus.

If you've used Scripture Union's holiday club material in the past, you'll notice this resource book looks and feels a little different.

We've tried to make this book as simple and concise as possible, with clear instructions for each day's programme that refer back to the overall club aims and objectives.

From the outset, this holiday club has been designed to help you connect with the 95% of children and young people not in church (information on adapting the content of each day for children who are already connected to church can be found on pages 23 and 24).

A NEW MODEL

The focus of Scripture Union's work is on the 95% of children and young people who are not in church (we'll refer to them as 'children from the 95' or 'the 95' from here on). So, we have written this holiday club material with these children as the target group.

We want to help you and your church to meet and journey with these children from them perhaps knowing very little about Jesus to being lifelong followers of him – though we don't expect that will all happen in the course of one holiday club!

This holiday club will allow your church to connect with children from the 95 and give them an opportunity to explore and respond to Jesus in appropriate ways, while also helping churched children (and young people working as helpers) to explore and respond further, and to grow in faith.

REVEALING JESUS

The Revealing Jesus mission framework is designed to help you journey into faith with the 95% of children and young people not in church.

We've identified four stages in the journey that most people follow as they engage with Christianity: **Connect**, **Explore**, **Respond** and **Grow**.

The framework provides shaping principles for each stage, but also offers flexibility in expression as we recognise that contexts, and children and young people themselves, vary hugely.

Find out more at: **https://content.scriptureunion.org.uk/revealingjesus**

We recommend that a holiday club is part of an integrated, ongoing strategy for mission and engagement with children from the 95. Even before you run this club, it would be good to consider what you might do next to develop the contacts you make through the event. We'll think more about that a little later, on page 28.

A DIFFERENT APPROACH

As a result of conversations with people who run holiday clubs, we recognise that families have busy lives and many churches are now running shorter clubs. So, we have provided material for three days in this book, with a further two days of material available online. The three-day outline here is complete, and the additional days are just that: they add to what is already in the book, but the programme works fine without them. One or both of the additional days can be added between Day 2 and Day 3 to make a longer club.

Other changes we have made to this material are to make it more appropriate for children from the 95.

Just for a moment, imagine yourself going to an event that you've never been to before. You don't know many, if any, people and the building is unfamiliar; you're not quite sure what happens, yet everyone else seems to know what to do, so it feels a bit threatening.

This might be the experience of children from the 95 coming to a holiday club. So, here are some of the things we have done:

UNDERSTANDING THE BASICS

Services

There are no outlines for a Sunday service. Although it's important to link children into a church, that often takes time. A service at the end of a holiday club week will be very unfamiliar to children from the 95, not least because it will be very different from the club. Instead, and at a different time, you might organise a family activity to which holiday club and church families all come, giving them the chance to build friendships with one another.

Stories

The material focuses on Gospel stories that might be very familiar to churched children but not to children from the 95. As we have turned things on their head, you may find it helpful to read the section on working with the 5% on pages 23 and 24.

Storytelling and drama

We have provided a range of options for sharing the passage from the Bible each day: an MP3 audio story, an animation, a straightforward reading of the relevant pages from *Diary of a Disciple: Luke's Story* or these pages performed as a drama. You may want to use the same method every day or use a variety of styles. The outline does not include a humorous drama.

Singing

We haven't suggested that you have a band and sing with the children, as it would be inappropriate to ask children who know little about Jesus to sing worship songs. However, children do love singing, so if you know good songs that don't require children to sing things they may not yet believe, you could use some of those. Teach them well and explain what the words mean simply and clearly.

Learning styles

We have adopted the **Explore Together** method of Bible discovery, in which children choose activities that suit their style of learning – whether that be hearing, seeing, talking, listening, doing or simply being quiet – and use these to help them think about and explore the Bible passage more.

In this approach, up to six different Zones are set up, and each child chooses which they will use to help them to explore and think about questions arising from that day's theme. Each day there will be a Question of the Day that will help the children to think about the passage, and then further questions that will help them to explore it. This exploring is self-led, and the leaders are there to help, not to impose activities.

More information on **Explore Together** and the individual Zones is given on pages 9 and 10.

Refreshments

During 'Exploring the story' you should serve refreshments. You will need to have a pause in some activities to make this possible; remember that younger children can take a long time to get through a drink and fruit or biscuit, so may need to sit out a little longer while a game restarts, for example. However, bear in mind that some children will move between Zones and may therefore catch on to the fact that it might be possible to get double rations this way. Work out a system to monitor who has had refreshments already!

UNDERSTANDING THE BASICS

 EXPLORE TOGETHER

What is the idea behind **Explore Together**?

Imagine for a moment a large bowl filled with jelly beans. The bowl is passed around and you are invited to take a handful. What is the next thing you do with the colourful sweets in your hand?

Do you sort them into colour groups? Eat them in a set order? Avoid a particular flavour completely? Or do you just open your mouth and throw them right in without any thought or reason?

It may be that you just don't like jelly beans; perhaps you're not in the mood for jelly beans and would have preferred the option of chocolate. You can discover a lot about a person by the way they eat or don't eat their jelly beans.

Using this analogy helps us understand how people of all faiths and none engage with the Bible. The diversity of human experience means that we all engage in very different ways. And yet, Bible engagement is so often presented in a 'one-size-fits-all' way. It's like handing out the jelly beans and only allowing people to eat the cinnamon ones.

Whenever we draw a group of people together we create an environment of wonder, creativity and diversity. Together we are a beautiful collection of artists, scholars, reflectors, dancers, data collectors, fact finders, readers, sculptors, writers, musicians, actors, talkers, listeners and more.

The children attending your holiday club will be just such a diverse collection. Explore Together makes the Bible accessible for everyone to engage with from their own unique starting point, in their own unique way, but within the safety of a community of explorers.

What are the different ways of exploring?

Explore Together defines six different exploring Zones:

Word Zone
For those who learn by reading. Items in this Zone could include: printed words from songs, prayers and stories, pens, paper, pencils, rulers, storybooks, Bibles.

Colour Zone
For those who learn by seeing, using shapes, colours, patterns and pictures. Items in this Zone could include: images, videos, paint, chalk, crayons, flags, ribbons.

Busy Zone
For those who learn by doing, using the ability to move around. For this Zone, we have provided instructions for a game.

Quiet Zone
For those who learn by reflecting, using a comfortable, quiet space where they will be undisturbed.

Chat Zone
For those who learn by thinking aloud, talking to others. This Zone simply needs a knowledgeable and confident Zone Guide, and, if possible, helpers, who will facilitate and encourage discussion.

Listening Zone
For those who learn by hearing, using words, music and poetry. Items in this Zone could include: tablets set up to play the Guardians of Ancora story quests and MP3 players.

What activities should I set up in each Zone? There don't seem to be any instructions.

The idea of **Explore Together** is that the children should decide for themselves what to do/make/read/write/listen to/talk or think about. There are no set activities and the role of the Zone Guides is to encourage the children to explore the Question of the Day for themselves, in whatever way they want to respond to it. The only exception to this is the Busy Zone, where we have given instructions for a game to play.

Do the children visit each Zone in turn?

No! Encourage the children to choose which Zone or Zones to visit, according to their own preferences. Some children will stay with one Zone for the whole of your club, some will visit two or three and some will go around everything. Allow the children to spend as much or as little time as they want in the Zones they visit.

Won't it all be very chaotic?

It is chaotic in the sense that the children are engaging in different ways. The explore Zones are designed to embrace a range of learning preferences. Children will very quickly find their own preferred activity and become occupied. Although there might be a buzz in the room, activity will be purposeful, colourful and appealing, and every child has the freedom to move around and make choices in a safe and supportive environment.

OVERVIEW AND BIBLE PROGRAMME

WHO DO YOU SAY I AM?

This holiday club invites children to explore who Jesus is. Each day unpacks a little of his story, beginning with the traditional Christmas narrative on Day 1, moving on to explore some of Jesus' teachings and miracles on Day 2 (and the additional days), leading up to and concluding with the Easter story.

The aim is that, over the course of the holiday club, the children are better equipped to answer Jesus' question, 'Who do you say I am?' (Luke 9:20) for themselves.

BIBLE DAY BY DAY

Day 1
Who is Jesus?
- Luke 1:1–56; 2:1–40
- *Diary of a Disciple: Luke's Story* pages 2–11 and 18–31

Exploring: the traditional Christmas story – the visit of the Angel Gabriel to Zechariah and then Mary; Mary's visit to Elizabeth; the census and Mary and Joseph's journey to Bethlehem; the birth of Jesus; the visit of the shepherds; meeting Simeon and Anna at the Temple.

Naturally, the activities that form part of Day 1 have a Christmas theme – which, unless you're running your holiday club at Christmas, will feel a little out of place. But, through this unexpected revisiting of the Christmas story, the children will have the opportunity to explore it afresh, aside from all the usual Christmas mayhem!

Day 2
What did Jesus do and say?
- Luke 5:1–32
- *Diary of a Disciple: Luke's Story* pages 70–88

Exploring: the call of the disciples; the miraculous catch of fish; the healing of a man with leprosy; the Pharisees' reaction to Jesus; the healing and forgiveness of the man who was lowered through a hole in a roof; Jesus calling Levi to follow him.

Although the story for Day 2 is quite long, it introduces many aspects of what Jesus did and said – including miracles, healings, teachings and interactions with those who wanted to follow him and those who really didn't like him at all.

Day 3
What happened to Jesus?
- Luke 22:1–24,39–54,63–71; 23:1–5,13–46,50–56; 24:1–31
- *Diary of a Disciple: Luke's Story* pages 302–307, 310–314, 317–323, 325–333 and 335–345

Exploring: the celebration of the Passover; the Last Supper, the betrayal and arrest of Jesus; Jesus' trial before Pilate; the crucifixion, the death and resurrection of Jesus, concluding with the disciples on the road to Emmaus.

Although the references listed above make this presentation of the Easter story seem as though it is made up of many tiny parts, the ways in which the story can be presented ensure that children are able to capture the whole narrative. At the end of this day, children will be invited to pause and reflect on how they would answer Jesus' question from Luke 9:20 – 'Who do you say I am?' – for themselves.

ADDITIONAL DAYS (online only)

If you wish to run your holiday club for four or five days, extra content enabling you to do this can be found online at su.org.uk/DiaryHolidayClub.

We recommend that the Additional Day(s) are inserted into the programme between Day 2 and Day 3 – thus expanding the amount of time children spend exploring what Jesus said by looking at his teaching about our interaction with others and with God. You can do either or both of the Additional Days: they stand alone, but add to the overall understanding of who Jesus is.

Additional Day 1
What did Jesus say about me and other people?
- Luke 10:25–37
- *Diary of a Disciple: Luke's Story* pages 168–171

Exploring: the story of the good Samaritan, helping children to understand something of the culture in which Jesus lived and ministered.

The activities and discussions that form part of Additional Day 1 will help children explore issues of social justice, social action and living differently that arise from the teachings of Jesus in the story of the good Samaritan.

Additional Day 2
What did Jesus say about me and God?
- Luke 11:1–13
- *Diary of a Disciple: Luke's Story* pages 174–176

Exploring: Jesus' teaching on prayer (including the Lord's Prayer) and discovering what Jesus said about the Holy Spirit.

The activities and discussions that form part of Additional Day 2 will help children explore what prayer is, how to pray and who the Holy Spirit is and what he (or she) does.

THE PROGRAMME

An outline of the suggested programme is given in the table on page 14 and described briefly below.

The Days, starting on page 29, give you activity material for each of these elements, for the three core Days of the club. Material for two Additional Days is available online at su.org.uk/DiaryHolidayClub.

The material will last for about two and a quarter hours, in a mixture of all-together, Zone and small-group time, but can be adapted to suit your context and the children you are working with.

PROGRAMME ELEMENTS

Team preparation

This is spiritual preparation for the team rather than practicalities, which should have been done first: talking about the day's passage and praying for the club.

Registration

Check in children and register any new children; deal with any parental questions.

Small group welcome

An activity and discussion in small groups as the children arrive and settle in.

Setting the scene

Any announcements for the day are made; a fun sketch or activity gets the children thinking about the day's topic.

Sharing the story

The material offers you a choice of four ways to present the day's Bible passage: audio, animation, drama or read aloud from *Diary of a Disciple: Luke's Story*.

Everybody active!

Lead the children in appropriate exercises. This could be led by Luke (it could be called 'Luke's Leaps') or another leader (perhaps as 'Diarists' Dance Moves').

Exploring the story

An opportunity for each child to choose one or more ways to explore the theme in more detail. Refreshments can also be served during this time.

Talk and make

Listening to what each child has discovered, drawing things together and making something as you talk.

Journal time

Continued discovery about the Day's passage and theme through puzzles and activities in an age-appropriate booklet.

Chat until children collected

A chance to complete any outstanding activity or puzzles until the children are collected.

Team debrief and clearing up

The team pause to debrief the session and pray for the children.

THE PROGRAMME

PROGRAMME TIMETABLE

TIMING	ACTIVITY	CHILDREN	TEAM
BEFORE CLUB BEGINS			
20 mins	Team preparation		All Team
15 mins	Registration	Individually	Registration team
CLUB BEGINS			
Small-group time			
15 mins	Small group welcome	Small groups	Group Leaders and Helpers
Together time			
20 mins	Setting the scene	All together	Presenters
15 minutes	Sharing the story	All together	Presenters
10 mins	Everybody active!	All together	Leader or Presenters
Zone time			
30 mins	Exploring the story	In Zones	Zone Guides
Small-group time			
30 mins	Talk and make	Small groups	Group Leaders and Helpers
15 minutes	Journal time	Small groups	Group Leaders and Helpers
AFTER CLUB			
10 mins	Children are collected	Small groups	Group Leaders and Helpers
20 mins	Team debrief and clearing up		All Team

THE PROGRAMME

EVERY DAY ITEMS

Each Day contains a list of specific items needed for that Day's activities. The following list of items will be needed for each Day:

Team preparation
- the Question of the Day and other questions (available to download)
- Bibles

Registration
- registration form
- consent form
- collection slips
- registers
- small group allocation list
- pens
- sticky labels

Small group welcome
- string
- scissors
- sticky tape
- colouring pens/pencils
- glue sticks
- a group box (large cardboard or plastic box) for storing your materials and journals during the club

Setting the scene
- two armchairs or smaller chairs

Sharing the story
- any equipment – depending on the method you are using
- a copy of *Diary of a Disciple: Luke's Story*

Everybody active!
- appropriate, pre-recorded music with a good beat, and a way to play this so that it can be heard

Exploring the story
- refreshments
- copies of the Question of the Day and other questions for each Zone (available to download)
- items needed each Day for the different Zones:

 Word Zone
- copies of *Diary of a Disciple: Luke's Story*
- some or all of the following books: *The Lion Storyteller Bible*, Good News Bible, International Children's Bible; Bible handbooks or commentaries open at the appropriate page
- sticky notes
- pens
- pencils
- lined paper
- small notebooks

 **Colour Zone**
- A4 paper
- felt-tip pens
- scissors
- glue sticks
- pencils

 Busy Zone
- a safe, reasonably sized space

 Quiet Zone
- a selection of pictures from the day's image collection (available to download)
- copies of *Diary of a Disciple: Luke's Story*, *The Lion Storyteller Bible*, Good News Bible, International Children's Bible
- pens and paper
- cushions or bean bags

 Chat Zone
- bean bags or cushions

Listening Zone
- tablets
- tablet holders
- MP3 players

Talk and Make
- copies of the Question of the Day and other questions (available to download)
- small whiteboard and marker (or clipboard and paper plus pen)
- colouring pens and pencils

Journal time
- copies of the appropriate journals *Day Book* or *Jotter*, for each child
- pens and felt-tip pens or colouring pencils

Going home
- paper
- colouring pens and pencils

TEAM ROLES

To run your holiday club, you'll need to recruit a team of willing and able volunteers who will be able to take responsibility for various aspects of your programme. Everyone must be recruited in line with your organisation's safer recruitment and safeguarding policies.

You will also need to refer to the adult-to-child ratios as described in your safeguarding policy to determine how many volunteers you will need. (Remember that any young leaders under the age of 18 count as children.) You may find it helpful to set a limit on the number of children who can attend – determined by how many volunteers you are able to recruit. Alternatively, you may have a good idea of how many children and young people you are expecting to attend and recruit your team based on these numbers.

Of course, depending on the size of your holiday club, you may find that one person on your team can hold several roles at the same time. For example, as mentioned below, Zone Guides could also be part of your Registration team.

Every team member should wear a badge that clearly identifies them and their role. Children should also wear name badges at all times. (Name badges should be removed at the end of the club session each day and kept securely at the venue.) Any adult or child who is seen on site and is not wearing an appropriate badge should be challenged.

CORE ROLES

The following roles are needed to ensure that your holiday club is a success.

Registration team

You will need several team members who can take responsibility for registering the children and young people on each day of your club. You will need to ensure that you do this in line with the advice given in your safeguarding policy and data protection policy. Although members of the Registration team may be able to fulfil other volunteer roles (such as Zone Guides), they cannot be Group Leaders or Group Helpers – as, once children are registered, they will need to be sent straight to their small group. The Registration team will also need to keep an accurate record of which team members are there each day, and which leaders and helpers are with which group.

Group Leaders and Group Helpers

Group Leaders and Group Helpers will work with the same small group of children over the course of the holiday club. They will work to create a team atmosphere within their small group and take time to have meaningful conversations together. Group Leaders are those with overall responsibility for the children and young people in their group and should be over 18 – as described in your safeguarding policy. Group Helpers are those who are under 18 (but over the upper age limit for your club), and therefore not taking direct responsibility for the children in the small group (when working out adult-to-child ratios for the club they are counted as children). Group Helpers are there to assist Group Leaders with their tasks and to work alongside them during small-group time.

Presenters

Two upfront Presenters lead some of the all-together time during the club. These should be two leaders who are confident when standing in front of a group of children and young people. They will need to set the scene for each day, share the story (using whichever method they prefer from the options provided) and may be the ones to run the 'Everybody active!' section, or at least to be joining in at the front as good examples.

Zone Guides

Zone Guides will be present in each Zone when children are exploring the story. You will need at least one Guide per Zone – although it is likely that Group Leaders and/or members of your Registration team will be able to take on the role of Zone Guide.

- In the Chat Zone the Zone Guide will need to facilitate unscripted conversations about the Question of the Day and other questions that are being explored. The Chat Zone would also benefit from having at least one leader who is skilled at talking with children who have problems. Some may have important or difficult things they want to talk about, but may not know how to begin the conversation. Each day, the Zone Guide here should remind the children that they can just say 'I want some help' and a leader will know they want to talk about something important, and will help them (in line with your organisation's safeguarding policy).
- In the Word and Colour Zones, Zone Guides are simply there to help children if needed, and perhaps to ask the children which question they are thinking about as they engage with the materials in the Zone. They are not there to direct the children or to offer a prescribed activity.
- In the Listening Zone the Zone Guide will need to be able to offer advice on using the various devices and playing the Guardians of Ancora quest.
- The Busy Zone Guide needs to be able to organise and run team games efficiently.
- In the Quiet Zone the Zone Guide will need to be able to gently enforce the quiet atmosphere.

Information for Zone Guides for each of the Zones is available to download.

OTHER ROLES

First aid

You will need to ensure that you have at least one qualified first aider available at all times during your holiday club. Please refer to your church's health and safety policy for advice on numbers of first aiders required at your event.

Safeguarding

You will also need to ensure that every member of your team is aware of who will function as the Safeguarding Lead for your holiday club, and that all team members are trained appropriately in accordance with your safeguarding policy.

Drama team

If you choose to tell the *Diary of a Disciple* stories using the drama scripts provided online, you will need to allocate members of your team to play the required parts. Of course, some overlap will be possible with team members who are in other roles, but you may find that some extra volunteers will be necessary for this. It might help to have the same person take on the role of Luke every day. This person might also lead the 'Everybody active!' session as Luke.

Refreshments team

The best time to serve refreshments will be when the children are in Zones. You will need a team to have prepared refreshments ready for this time, who can then take them to the children as appropriate. This could be done by Group Helpers if you don't have enough for a separate team. As children could be moving between Zones, you will need to keep a check on who has had refreshments and who hasn't!

SMALL GROUPS

The children will spend a lot of time in a small group. These should be so much more than a method for managing large numbers of children: rather, they are an opportunity for leaders and helpers to develop appropriate, healthy and meaningful relationships with their group members.

LEADING GOOD SMALL GROUPS AND DEVELOPING RELATIONSHIPS

Group dynamics can be tricky at a holiday club, both if few children know each other and if lots know each other really well! The Group Leader will need to help quiet children to participate in ways that are appropriate for them while making sure those who talk a lot allow others a chance to speak. But, as the children and leaders get to know one another, these can be great times of fun.

Moving on from favourite colours…

A holiday club provides an incredible opportunity to connect with children and help them explore the Bible and encounter Jesus. Throughout the time at holiday club there are plenty of moments to talk with children, get to know them and ask questions. It's easy to think that all the spiritual input happens through the story and prayers, or from the upfront Presenters. But those moments of conversation around the table, over craft or during games can be very meaningful, if approached with purpose.

Often when speaking with children at holiday club it can be easy to stay on the safe topics – favourite colours, holiday destinations, schoolteachers and lessons – but holiday club provides a prime opportunity to truly connect, go deeper and facilitate real thinking and reflection. Try to take those moments of conversation, wherever they are, to ask questions that open further discussion about life, God, Jesus, faith, church and more. But how?

Pray as a team for boldness and opportunities. Encourage one another with stories of conversations at the end of the day.

Ask questions and follow up with 'why?' Fight the urge to tell the 'right' answer. This is about encouraging the children to explore. Allow the children the chance to settle in and get used to the club and their group, but as they do, begin to ask questions, such as:

- Have you ever been to church?
- Do you think there is a God?
- What is most important to you?
- If there is a God, what do you think God would be like?
- Who do you think Jesus is – a made-up character, a good person, a teacher, God's Son?
- Do you think it's important to believe in God?

Make sure that the children don't feel bombarded by questions. Some children will assume there are 'right' answers to these questions and, as they get to know you, will want to please you by what they say. Make it clear that it's OK if the answer to 'have you ever been to church?' is 'no' – you will still like them!

Share something of who you are and what you believe. Keep it short, keep it brief, keep it child-friendly, keep it positive and allow questioning of what has been said. You might talk about:

- what your response to the above questions would be
- a short, appropriate story from your life where you see God helping you
- why you believe in Jesus as your Lord and Saviour
- how faith in God shapes your life
- why you think a church family is important
- a time when God answered your prayer
- a time when God didn't answer a prayer in a way you expected, but you still believe he answered it.

Opening up the story

Encourage the children to engage with the story on a deeper level, not just as a memory or comprehension exercise. Try not to stifle responses or creative thinking or 'wrong theology'. Allow thought and imagination to flow as a conversation, and ask more questions when a child answers. 'How did you get to that conclusion?' is a great follow-up. You might also ask:

- Why do you think it happened like that?
- What would you have thought/said/felt if you had been one of the characters in the story?
- Is there anything that confuses you in the story? Why?
- What do you think would happen next?
- What does this story tell us about God/Jesus?
- Does this story make you think differently about God/Jesus?

It might feel awkward to begin with, or perhaps fear tells us conversation will fall flat or go nowhere. But what if these conversations could change the course of a life? What if these conversations could encourage a child to really think about responding to Jesus or even exploring more by coming to your next event? What if these moments allow children to grapple with deeper things while having an incredible time at holiday club? That's a risk worth taking!

PREPARING YOUR VENUE

The time you ask your team to arrive before each session begins will depend on how much preparation you expect to do prior to the children arriving. If you have decorated your venue in advance (and are able to leave it decorated for the duration of your club) you will have less daily preparation to do. If you are not able to decorate in advance, your daily preparation time will be longer.

REGISTRATION AND COLLECTION AREA

This area would most logically be placed near the entrance to your venue.

Ideally, the children arriving at your club will have been registered in advance, and you will already have their consent forms. Practically, there will always be children who arrive who need to be registered on the day. If you are able to set up an area for those already registered and an area for those who need to register on the day, this will help to avoid long queues before the day begins.

Make sure that, when the registration desk closes, all forms are moved to a safe place where they can be accessed easily if needed, but only by team members and not by any parents leaving late or arriving early.

UPFRONT AREA

Your upfront area is the place where the Presenters will be when leading all-together time, where the story will be told from and where the story drama (if you are using drama) will take place.

There needs to be space from which all the children attending your club will be able to see and hear the Presenters and anyone else. If the children are sitting on the floor, they will be able to see best if the Presenters are standing at floor level. If the children are sitting on chairs, you may need to create some staging so that the Presenters can be seen better.

Make this area look attractive with bunting, or by draping coloured fabrics, or creating a backdrop.

At the beginning of each day your Presenters will give notices, share plans for the day and deliver a short sketch. This will help to set the scene for the rest of the day's activities. If possible, your upfront area should include two armchairs, which will feature in some of the sketches at the beginning of each day.

DAILY DECORATIONS FOR THE UPFRONT AREA AND VENUE

If you are able to decorate your venue differently each day, the following themes and ideas are suggested:

Day 1

The first day of the *Diary of a Disciple: Luke's Story* holiday club has a Christmas theme. So, where possible, you should decorate your venue accordingly. Members of your team or the wider church will probably have Christmas decorations you can borrow – and some may have artificial Christmas trees that would cause a stir by being used out of season!

Day 2

Items that show allegiance to a team, club or school, such as scarves, shirts, caps, rosettes etc. Have as many different teams as possible on display so as not to favour one over others.

Day 3

'Goodbye' bunting. Print or write out the letters on individual sheets of paper and peg these to a washing line – hang one across the stage and, if possible, place more copies elsewhere in your venue.

Additional Day 1

As for Day 2, but during 'Setting the scene' one of the Presenters will quietly take down all but their team's colours/scarves etc. Make sure this can be done without fuss or needing ladders!

Additional Day 2

Several washing lines of images illustrating prayer and communication, including listening, such as a mobile phone, megaphone, praying hands, ear etc.

SMALL GROUP AREAS

You may choose to give each small group a name, number or colour. The children will make decorations for their small group area on the first day. Create shields, posters or flags to represent the group. Unless you have enough space for a separate 'making area' (see below) in the venue, think about whether the children can do their making activities and fill in their journals on the floor in the group area, or if you need a table for each group. (If space is an issue, think about not using chairs, which take up a lot of room.)

EXPLORE ZONES

With some careful thought and planning, all six Zones can work in one large space. Alternatively, you may choose to spread the Zones around your building providing you can adequately supervise them. You may also want to consider running fewer Zones if your space simply won't work with all six. Some Zones need more room than others, and some can be scaled down to be relatively small.

Depending on your space, you should prepare your Zone spaces in advance – this could be full set-up of each dedicated space, or it could be preparing a box that can be quickly unpacked into a multi-use space at the appropriate time.

 The **Word Zone** will have a number of books available for the children to read. Do you want these on the floor or on tables?

 The **Colour Zone** will include the use of colouring pens and modelling materials; it would benefit from having tables, if possible, or perhaps a large plastic sheet on the floor.

 The **Busy Zone** will need a large, safe space. This can be indoors or outdoors (but you will need a wet weather plan if outdoors).

 The **Quiet Zone** needs to be in a quieter area. It would benefit from some floor cushions, bean bags or low chairs.

 The **Chat Zone** would benefit from some floor cushions or low chairs where children and leaders can chat together easily.

 The **Listening Zone** might benefit from cushions too. If you are using tablets in the Listening Zone, it might be helpful to keep these on tables and have them in tablet holders so that they don't get put down on the floor and then trodden on accidentally. Remember that devices need to have parental controls in place so that children cannot access anything unsuitable on the internet, and that if you have borrowed these from people, the children should not be able to access personal documents or emails.

Making area

If you have enough space, you could set up tables for each group so that, during 'Talk and make', they can work on their craft away from their group area. You can then have everything laid out ready for each day.

However, this could spoil the flow of conversation when unpacking what the children have discovered in the Explore Zones, as they would have to move from one place to another. And, of course, you may not have enough space for a separate area.

Another option is to put everything needed for that day's making activity in a bag or box for each group – or even pack up small paper carriers with exactly what is needed for each child – and take these to the groups as the 'Talk and make' time approaches.

ADAPTING YOUR CLUB

CHILDREN WITH ADDITIONAL NEEDS

The term 'additional needs' covers a wide spectrum of issues. Each child with additional needs coming to your club will benefit from you thinking through what will help them as an individual to get the best from it. Here are a few examples to help you think about what might need doing:

- Those with physical disabilities may need adaptations to certain activities such as games or the table at which they make things, or larger print for those with visual issues.
- Children with autism will benefit from being told each day what is happening in the programme, and may need a printed schedule with verbal updates if last-minute changes are made.
- A child with learning disabilities may need to be in a younger age group if they can't cope with the level at which their peers are talking.
- A child in foster care might not need any special adaptations (apart from not appearing in any photographs of the activities) but would benefit from their group leader being aware of their circumstances.

If you use a pre-booking system for children and become aware that a child with additional needs is coming to the club, contact their parent or carer and ask what you can do to help them get the best out of the club. Make sure you have enough team members to assign a one-to-one carer, if needed. If a child simply turns up on the day to register, make sure you have a conversation with the person who brings them about what extra or different help they might need, and check back with them during the week.

CHILDREN FROM A 5% BACKGROUND

If you have used a Scripture Union holiday club resource book before, you will be used to reading a paragraph about how to help children with no church background to get the best from the club. But now, as we are focusing on these children (the 95), you will need to think briefly about the 5% or so of children in your community who do have a connection with church and may come to your club! They may make up more than 5% of the children in your club, but you should still make everything appropriate and accessible to those with no church background.

ADAPTING YOUR CLUB

Children from the 5% are probably comfortable coming to church; they will probably know the Gospel narratives used in the club; they may be there a long time before and after other children because their parent is involved on the team. So how do you help them to still have a great time?

If you know the children well, it would be great to help them understand why there has been this shift of focus. In advance of the club, explain the importance of giving children who don't come to church the opportunity to hear about Jesus. Ask them to pray for those who will come, and for God to work in their lives. Help them to think about some of the things they can do to make this work: inviting their friends to come to the club, listening to the stories without interrupting and saying they know what comes next (*really* listening – they might learn something new!), not always answering the questions immediately without giving others chance to think, and so on. Reassure them they will still enjoy it, and that you still want them there; encourage them to talk in their groups about what Jesus means to them. They can be peer evangelists!

But they are still children, and may find it hard when they aren't allowed to shine with their Bible knowledge. Think carefully about whether it's better to spread the 5% children between groups, or to put them in a group together so they can focus on growing in their faith rather than exploring.

CHILDREN FROM OTHER FAITHS

Because the focus of this club is on children who are not from a church background, in one sense there is no need to make special provision for children of other faiths. You will be speaking in words and ways that are understandable to children who are not of the Christian faith. But it will be important that you explain carefully certain truths about Jesus. Some faiths will respect him as a prophet but no more, while others will recognise numerous gods, not just one. Be honest and open in your publicity that this is a Christian club, so that any parent who sends their child knows they will hear Bible stories.

Think ahead about the words you use, the things you ask children to do and the questions they might raise because of their experiences of another faith; be ready to respect what they say as their experience and belief. Avoid making sweeping statements or judgements about their faith or how some who follow it live their lives. Pray for the Holy Spirit to work in them, as it is his role to convince them of who Jesus is, not ours. And in your enthusiasm for a child to know Jesus, don't encourage any to make a decision that would put them in conflict with their family.

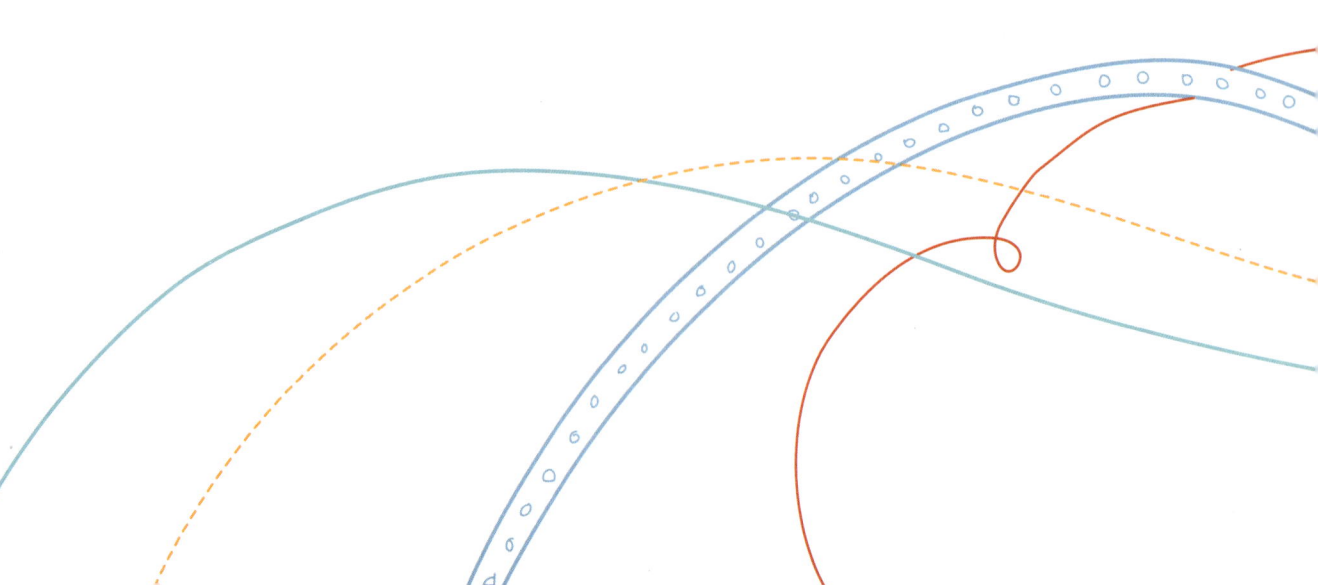

A NOTE ON REGISTRATION AND COLLECTION

If possible, encourage parents and carers to complete booking forms in advance of your club. These should then be returned to the leader of the holiday club, school office or community group leader, depending on how you make contact with families. This means you can allocate children to small groups in advance, and you will already be aware of any dietary requirements, medical issues and physical, educational or behavioural special needs. Remember to check these when planning your club activities and allocating team.

In some contexts pre-registering is not practical, so you will need to ensure that you have plenty of volunteers who are able to help greet the children and their parents or carers each day, providing them with the registration form to fill in. **Children should not attend the event unless written permission has been given**.

Make sure all data is collected in accordance with your organisation's GDPR policy.

Registration can be a lengthy process, so you might choose to open your doors earlier on the first day of your club. On subsequent days you may want to adapt your registration process so those who registered previously are fast-tracked, while making space for any new children to be registered.

You will need to keep accurate daily lists of who is in which group in case of fire or other emergencies, especially should you need to evacuate the building when the children are scattered in Zones. Each Group Leader should have an up-to-date list of who is in their group each day.

Make sure you have a clear plan of what you would do in case of an emergency, and where the children would congregate outside. Presenters should explain this to the children on the first day: keep this clear but light, so as not to worry children.

ADDITIONAL RESOURCES

ADDITIONAL DAYS

This holiday club resource book contains three half-day sessions that will form a complete three-day holiday club. For those who wish to run a four- or five-day club, two additional half-day sessions are available at **su.org.uk/DiaryHolidayClub**.

Each session works independently of the others, but care will need to be taken to ensure that children understand the context of the story they are exploring in terms of the overarching narrative around Jesus' life.

BOOKLETS FOR CHILDREN

Day Book
For younger children

This 32-page booklet contains text from *Diary of a Disciple: Luke's Story*, along with small-group material, puzzles and activities, for younger children.

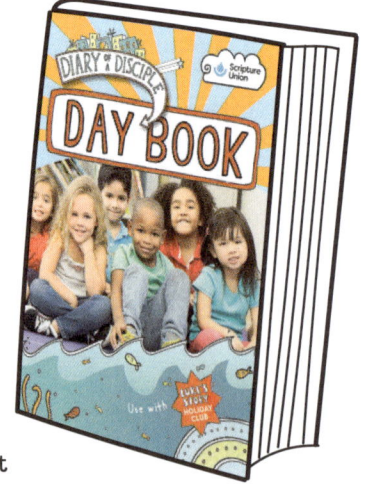

Jotter
For older children

This 48-page booklet contains text from *Diary of a Disciple: Luke's Story*, along with small-group material, puzzles and activities. It is ideal for use with 8 to 11s.

ADDITIONAL RESOURCES

ANIMATIONS AND AUDIO STORIES

Video animations and audiobook files of each of the stories included in this holiday club are available from su.org.uk/DiaryHolidayClub. The animations and audio files range in length from 5 to 8 minutes, depending on which story is being told.

DRAMA SCRIPTS

Drama scripts that retell each of the stories included in this holiday club are available to download from su.org.uk/DiaryHolidayClub. These provide one of the storytelling options for 'Sharing the story'.

The drama scripts vary in length from 10 to 17 minutes and require a range of props and costumes for certain characters. If possible, have the same person take on Luke's role and narrate each day's story (as in the script) or, if necessary, you can use a different narrator for each day. If you do this, the script may need amending slightly.

You may wish to adapt the scripts slightly, depending on number of volunteers you have available in your team and the amount of time you have.

PUBLICITY

See the inside back cover for details of the *Diary of a Disciple: Luke's Story* holiday club publicity materials produced by Christian Publicity and Outreach. (Please note, CPO resources are not available through Scripture Union.)

OTHER DOWNLOADABLE RESOURCES

A range of downloads to help you run your club is available from su.org.uk/DiaryHolidayClub, including:

- printable versions of the photocopiable resources
- team roles
- Zone Guide notes
- Question of the Day
- Explore Together FAQs
- logos
- poster
- club aims form
- evaluation form

and lots more!

LEGAL REQUIREMENTS AND SAFEGUARDING

There are various legal requirements you will need to be familiar with and conform to as you prepare for your holiday club. Things to consider include:

- safeguarding and child protection policies
- safer recruitment policies and procedures
- provision of adequate space(s) in your venue
- meeting adult-to-child ratios
- registering your club with any necessary authorities
- insurance
- data protection
- accidents and first aid
- issues of health and safety, including risk assessments
- fire procedures and guidelines
- food hygiene

To obtain up-to-date information on all of these requirements go to 'Legal requirements for running a club' at su.org.uk/DiaryHolidayClub.

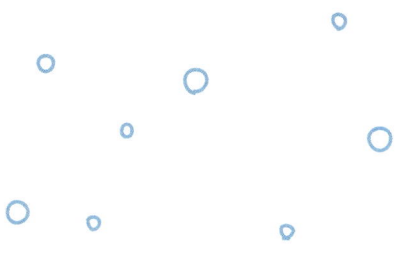

FOLLOW-ON

WHAT NEXT?

You may think this is a strange place to put a section about follow-on to the club, and there will be more about it at the end of the book – but your club will be far more effective if it's part of an ongoing strategy of work with children from the 95 than if it's just a once-a-year event.

If your *Diary of a Disciple: Luke's Story* holiday club has helped you to connect with children who don't come to church, then make sure you have some event or activity planned to take place not too long after the club ends so that you can build on these connections. It would be great if you could have another event within a month or so, before you've forgotten the children's names, or they have stopped writing things in the *Diary of a Disciple* style! It doesn't have to be a massive event: you could hold a games and pizza party, or a family activity afternoon. If it's planned in advance in terms of the type of activity, date and time, you can give children an invitation to it on the last day of the club.

You could also maximise the opportunities you've created by running something every four to six weeks, right through to next year's club. These events could tie in with special times such as harvest, bonfire night, Christmas, pancake day, Easter, one of the May bank holidays and perhaps a sporting event in early summer. Forward planning will enable you to build on each opportunity by advertising the next event, perhaps even saying 'tickets are available today!' even if a ticket isn't strictly necessary. They are far more likely to come if they have a ticket, rather than just an advert!

As children and perhaps their families come to events such as these, you'll need to think about how you take them along from that first connection and the exploration that they have done through the week on to the next step. Think in terms of moving them slightly on in the amount and depth you say about Jesus each time. There is more about this at the end of the book, on page 60.

You may decide to run a regular club as a result of your holiday club. It doesn't have to happen every week: regular could mean once a month, or the first and third Tuesday evenings/Saturday mornings, for example. You could run weekly clubs for half a term, such as six weeks after October half-term through almost to Christmas, and then from February half-term towards Easter for six weeks. You may find it easier to recruit team to help you if it's for a limited time: many people's busy lives mean they are reluctant to commit to something indefinitely. The same is probably true for parents who have to get their children to activities! There is material for a six-week after-school club, based on *Diary of a Disciple: Luke's Story* available to download free from the Scripture Union website.

It may be that, as you plan the holiday club, you can have others planning a programme for what follows. If your church is large enough, don't feel you and your team have to do everything: draw in others to be part of this exciting journey!

DIARY DAYS

WHO IS JESUS?

BIBLE PASSAGE
Luke 1:1–56; 2:1–40

DIARY OF A DISCIPLE: LUKE'S STORY
pages **2** to **11** and **18** to **31**

BEFORE YOUR CLUB BEGINS

Team preparation

Invite your team to gather together 20 minutes before registration begins, when the room is ready. This should not be a time for setting up your venue or completing last-minute preparations, rather a time to pause, reflect and pray together.

Talk together about the overall theme for the day (the birth of Jesus) and remind team members that today you will be using Christmas narratives.

Answer for yourselves the Question of the Day and the further questions. (Remind everyone that what they say in this time may not be appropriate to repeat to the children.) Pray for one another and for the club, the children and God's work in everyone.

Registration

As each child arrives, make sure your registration team are ready to greet them. If you were able to obtain registration and consent forms in advance, you will simply need to check off each child as they arrive and make appropriate arrangements for collection. Collection slips are available from su.org.uk/DiaryHolidayClub. If the children attending your club have not been pre-registered, you will need to ensure you have the time and the space for parents and carers to complete the relevant paperwork. No child should attend the club without permission.

Once each child is registered, allocate them to a small group and write their name and group name or number on a sticky label or name badge; give the label to the child for them to affix it to their clothing. If possible, allocate a few members of your registration team as 'welcomers' who can take the registered children to their small groups and introduce them to their leaders.

When registration is completed, remember that each Group Leader will need a list of the children in their group in case of emergency.

YOU WILL NEED

Items from the **Every Day** list on page 15 plus:

Small group welcome
- rolls of paper
- bamboo canes

Setting the scene
- Christmas jumpers
- Christmas hats
- Christmas music and the means to play it
- four wrapped Christmas presents each containing a different component of a traditional Christmas dinner
- a Christmas card in a sealed envelope containing a printed ultrasound image of a baby; the words on the envelope should say: 'The real Christmas gift'

Exploring the story

 Word Zone
- *Diary of a Disciple: Luke's Story* open at pages 2 to 11 and 18 to 31
- *The Lion Storyteller Bible* open at page 62 ('The First Christmas')
- Good News Bible or International Children's Bible open at Luke 1,2

 Colour Zone
- modelling clay or dough
- tissue paper
- A4 black paper
- a long piece of wallpaper to create a doodling area

 Busy Zone
- coloured cones (red, orange, blue, white)
- a selection of equipment such as small bean bags, soft balls, tennis balls, quoits

 Quiet Zone
- *Diary of a Disciple: Luke's Story* open at pages 2 to 11 and 18 to 31
- *The Lion Storyteller Bible* open at page 62 ('The First Christmas')
- Good News Bible or International Children's Bible open at Luke 1,2

 Listening Zone
- tablets ready to play Guardians of Ancora: Jesus is born
- MP3 players with *Diary of a Disciple: Luke's Story* audiobook chapter 1

Talk and make
- PVA glue
- glue dots or a glue gun (adult use only)
- scraps of fabric
- wooden lolly sticks
- half-size wooden lolly sticks
- gold stars
- ribbon or wool

DAY 1 Who is Jesus?

YOUR OUTLINE FOR DAY 1

Small-group time
15 minutes in small groups

Small group welcome (15 mins)

You will need:
- ☐ rolls of paper
- ☐ bamboo canes
- ☐ string

As the children arrive, make sure your team are ready to welcome them into their small groups. If possible, allocate a specific space for each small group that can become their group home for the duration of your club.

As each child joins the group, the team leaders and helpers should encourage them to decorate the group home space (and group box). If your space does not allow for a 'permanent' group home for the duration of the club, you could adapt this activity by encouraging the children to create banners, posters or other more moveable decorations.

As the children create, encourage your team leaders and helpers to introduce themselves and engage in positive, meaningful conversations. As this is the first time you have met the children, this is the occasion when you can talk about holidays, pets and colours as a way of getting to know one other and helping them to settle in!

Before 'Setting the scene' is due to begin, ask the children to help you put all of your unused decorating materials back in your 'group home' box.

Together time
45 minutes all together

Setting the scene (20 mins)

You will need:
- ☐ Christmas jumpers
- ☐ Christmas hats
- ☐ Christmas music and the means to play it
- ☐ four wrapped Christmas presents each containing a different component of a traditional Christmas dinner
- ☐ a Christmas card in a sealed envelope containing a printed ultrasound image of a baby; the words on the envelope should say: 'The real Christmas gift'

Today's session focuses on the birth of Jesus – the traditional Christmas story. If you have been able to decorate your venue using Christmas trees and Christmas decorations, it's likely the children will already be asking their small group leaders and helpers to explain why this is the case!

Your Presenters should be wearing Christmas jumpers and hats as they arrive on stage. If possible, play some Christmas music as they arrive. They should greet the children with a loud shout of 'Happy Christmas!' and sit down in their armchairs. They should then introduce themselves, formally welcome the children to the club and give any necessary health and safety announcements, including clear instructions about what to do if the fire alarm sounds.

Following this they should introduce today's theme using the points below – in as comedic a style as possible:

- Compare Christmas jumpers and hats (ending up swapping jumpers after a brief squabble).
- Share their favourite part of their annual Christmas celebrations, and invite a few children to do the same.

- Share their favourite Christmas song, and encourage the children to join in as they sing the first few lines, perhaps splitting the room in half and competing against one another at the same time.
- Give each other two gifts – containing different components of a traditional Christmas dinner (arguing over the fact that each person only has some of the required ingredients, trying to snatch back items from one another to make their own Christmas meal, resulting in a small food fight between the Presenters).
- After realising that Christmas dinner is no longer possible, as all the ingredients are destroyed, they find an unopened Christmas card that had previously been overlooked. On the envelope are the words 'The Real Christmas Gift'.
- They are confused but go quiet and open the card. An ultrasound scan of a baby is found in the card – and they briefly question whether either of them is trying to explain that they are having a baby. On realising this isn't the case, they concede that perhaps hearing today's story will help.

Sharing the story (15 mins)

There are four different ways of sharing the story each day. Feel free to mix and match these approaches or use the same format every day, if this will work better in your context.

It's important that the children know that the stories they hear or watch come from the Bible. Show a copy of *Diary of a Disciple: Luke's Story* and explain that it is based on the book in the Bible written by a man called Luke. Say that your story is a re-telling of Luke's book in the Bible and it really happened: this isn't a made-up story.

Option 1: Drama

A drama script re-telling today's story, based on the text from *Diary of a Disciple: Luke's Story* is available to download from su.org.uk/DiaryHolidayClub.

Option 2: Audio story

An MP3 audio file telling today's story (from the *Diary of a Disciple: Luke's Story* audiobook) is available to download from su.org.uk/DiaryHolidayClub.

Option 3: Animation

An MP4 video animation telling today's story is available to download from su.org.uk/DiaryHolidayClub.

Option 4: Reading aloud

Depending on your context, you may wish to have a storyteller each day who sits down and reads aloud the story from *Diary of a Disciple: Luke's Story* pages 2 to 11 and 18 to 31. This should be a volunteer from your team who is confident in reading aloud and will help the story to come alive as they read. You may wish to have the same storyteller for every session of your club, or you may prefer to have a different storyteller each day.

When the story has finished the Presenters should thank anyone who has helped to tell it, and comment on the incredible things that happened when Jesus was born. They should be excited about exploring this more!

Everybody active! (10 mins)

Lead the children in appropriate exercises.

Explain that most writers have to get up and do something energetic every so often, as it helps ideas to flow. This could be led by Luke (it could be called 'Luke's Leaps') or another leader (perhaps as 'Diarists' Dance Moves'.) You could use Christian songs for this, as long as you don't tell the children that they have to join in with the words. If you don't have anyone who could lead this, there are videos available on the internet with songs and movements that would work well for this, both Christian and secular. Check them before use and have the leader work out what movements they will do.

Zone time
30 minutes in Zones

Exploring the story (30 mins)

The Presenters should explain that everyone is going to explore the story, and there are lots of different ways of doing this. They should briefly describe the different Zones (using the explanations from page 9) and say there is an important question to think about:

WHO IS JESUS?

There are also some other questions:

- Why would God choose to be a baby?
- What difference does it make to people that God is with them?
- Have you ever known that God has been with you? When?

The Presenters should tell the children how long they have got to explore the story and say they can go to whichever Zone they like, and they can either stay there all the time or visit some other Zones too. (It's very important that the children are allowed to choose the Zone or Zones that works best for them.) Any child who is unsure of what to do or where to go should come to the front or ask their group leader for help. They then send the children off to Zones.

In the various Zones, invite the children to explore the questions which are printed out and displayed; Zone Guides should encourage the children to keep thinking about them. You will also be serving refreshments during this time; remember to keep a check on who has had them.

Word Zone

You will need:
- ☐ *Diary of a Disciple: Luke's Story* open at pages 2 to 11 and 18 to 31
- ☐ *The Lion Storyteller Bible* open at page 62 ('The First Christmas')
- ☐ Good News Bible or International Children's Bible open at Luke 1,2

Encourage the children to explore the different versions of the stories and to write down anything that strikes them as they think about the questions of the day.

Colour Zone

You will need:
- ☐ modelling clay or dough
- ☐ tissue paper
- ☐ A4 black paper
- ☐ a long piece of wallpaper to create a doodling area
- ☐ colouring pens and pencils

Encourage the children to explore the story through drawing or writing about it or creating models.

DAY 1 Who is Jesus?

 **Busy Zone**

You will need:
- ☐ coloured cones (red, orange, blue, white)
- ☐ a selection of equipment such as small bean bags
- ☐ soft balls
- ☐ tennis balls
- ☐ quoits

All change!

The idea of this game is for the leader to keep changing the priorities and aims as the children play. Just as angels came and shared a message from God that changed each character's priorities, so the leader will change the aim of the game.

Before the children arrive, set out the four coloured areas using your coloured cones, as shown in the diagram above.

Split the children into two teams and invite them to begin the game standing on either side of your playing area.

Before you start the game, explain how to play it:

- If you have the ball, you can't be touched and you can't move.
- If you do not have the ball, you are free to move anywhere, including inside coloured areas.
- If you have the ball you can only pass it to someone; there is no shooting or dribbling in this game.
- Score by passing the ball to a team member who is standing in the correct colour area. For example, Team 1 will score in the red area and Team 2 will score in the orange area.
- When a team scores, the ball is then given to a member of the other team to start from that area.

Tell each team which colour area is their scoring area, then start the game by giving a ball to one child. Encourage the children to play for a few minutes so they know what they are doing.

Call a halt and explain that, from now on, the rules will keep changing slightly. Sometimes a player will have to get a new item (ball/quoit/bean bag etc) from a leader; sometimes it will be the scoring area that changes. The game won't stop, so they must listen for your instructions, which will always begin with 'All change' being shouted.

From here on, every few minutes call 'All change' and make amendments such as the following, one at a time:

- Team 1 now scores in orange area, Team 2 scores in white area.
- You must make 5 passes before you can score.
- If you have the ball you must hop on the spot.
- You can only score with a quoit (or whatever item you have).

- Each team member must make a unique animal noise when they score.

Try to come up with your own rules; be creative and random. The idea is to create a sense of fun with a little healthy panic!

Pause and talk together:

- Who had fun?
- What was easy about this game? What was hard?
- Could you hear the leader's instructions through all the noise of the game?
- Did you manage to keep up with all the changes?
- Were you afraid of a change being made to the game?
- Do you think the changes were good?
- What do you think the shepherds/Mary/Zachariah felt when they received a new instruction?
- Question of the Day: Who is Jesus?

Conclude with the following words, or similar:

Just as the instructions in the game changed how we played, the messages the angels brought from God changed how these people lived their lives. I believe we can hear from God too, and hearing from God changes how we live our lives.

 Quiet Zone

You will need:
- ☐ *Diary of a Disciple: Luke's Story* open at pages 2 to 11 and 18 to 31
- ☐ *The Lion Storyteller Bible* open at page 62 ('The First Christmas')
- ☐ Good News Bible or International Children's Bible open at Luke 1,2

Around the walls of the space you are using have the Question of the Day, the extra questions and some of the pictures from the image collection displayed, and have the books available for any child who wants to read the passage again.

 Chat Zone

Chat with children about the story and questions. You may need to ask questions to get the conversation started, such as 'Which part of the story did you like best? Why?' But some children will just want to chat about anything and everything! Allow them to do so, as this builds strong relationships, but then focus the chat a little by asking them one or two questions about the story, including the Question of the Day. They need to know that you are genuinely interested in them and their lives, not just their response to the story.

You should also explain to the children that there may be things in their lives that they find difficult, or sad, and that they would like to talk about. If so, they can just say 'I want some help' and you or another leader will know they want to talk about something important, and will help them (in line with your organisation's safeguarding policy).

 Listening Zone

You will need:
- ☐ tablets ready to play Guardians of Ancora: Jesus is born
- ☐ MP3 players with *Diary of a Disciple: Luke's Story* audiobook chapter 1

Invite children to play the Guardians of Ancora quest on the tablets. Remind them that they can also do a quiz on the story once it's completed (you will need to show them where to find this). They can also listen to the audio story, if available, on devices.

You may need a few people available in this area to help children access quests or stories. This is an area where Group Helpers would probably excel! They will need to re-set the tablets – get each one ready at the start of the right quest again – if more than one child wants to play the quest.

At the end of 'Exploring the story', send the children back to their small groups. You may want to play some music to signify that the time is ending – perhaps start it quietly two to three minutes before the end of the time and turn the volume up slowly. This way Zone Guides will know to start winding up the activities and sending children back to their small groups, without having to watch the time!

Small-group time
45 minutes in small groups

Talk and make (30 mins)

You will need:
- ☐ PVA glue
- ☐ glue dots or a glue gun (adult use only)
- ☐ scraps of fabric
- ☐ wooden lolly sticks
- ☐ half-size wooden lolly sticks
- ☐ gold stars
- ☐ ribbon or wool

Invite the children to tell you what they did and what they discovered in the Explore Zones that helped them to answer the Question of the Day: 'Who is Jesus?'

Encourage the children to listen to one another. Write down what each child says, even if you disagree with it, using the whiteboard (or clipboard and paper). Add in your own answer, perhaps doing this first to set the example. Be ready to gently correct anything that is wildly inaccurate (see pages 18 and 19 for more about how and why).

Move on to the day's making activity while keeping the discussion going. Explain that what they make will help them to remember today's story, and to keep on thinking about the Question of the Day. Discuss the extra questions for the day, though you don't need to write down all the answers to these. Group Leaders should not make this conversation a formal question and answer session; rather, they should aim to keep the atmosphere as relaxed as possible. Further questions for the children to explore today are: 'Why would God choose to be a baby? Have you ever known that God has been with you? When? What difference does it make to people that God is with them?

Stick stable

1. Give each child three small lolly sticks or half sticks and encourage them to draw a face on each one, for Joseph, Mary and Jesus.

2. Show them how to wrap the sticks in fabric and stick this on with PVA glue.

3. Invite the children to make a stable shape using five larger lolly sticks (two for the roof, two for walls and one for the base). Help them to stick their stable together using either glue dots or the glue gun (PVA will not be strong enough).

3 Again using either the glue gun or glue dots, invite them to stick Joseph and Mary either side of Jesus on the back of the bottom of the stable.

4 Give each child a star to stick at the top of the stable on the front, and a loop of wool or ribbon to stick on the back to hang it up.

5 Suggest the children write 'He is Christ the Lord' along the two roof sticks, with the reference Luke 2:11.

Journal time (15 mins)

Clear away the craft materials. Give each child a copy of the *Day Book* (younger children) or *Jotter* (older children). Invite them to spend some time completing pages 5 to 9 (*Day Book*) or pages 6 to 11 (*Jotter*) as they reflect on all that they have discovered today.

When your club ends
30 minutes

Children are collected (10 mins)

Each day, the Presenters' Challenge is to draw a picture that illustrates one of the stories from that day, or to re-tell of one of the stories in the style of Luke's diary (but not just copying what's in the book!), or to make a diary entry about their own day in the style of Luke's diary.

Explain that the Presenters have set the children a challenge, and explain what it is. Say that the challenge is optional, it's not homework, but if any child wants to do it they should bring their entry, with their name on, tomorrow, and hand it in to you.

As you wait for parents and carers to collect their children, invite them to complete some of the extra pages in their *Day Book* or *Jotter*. Alternatively, they could work on further decoration of your group home area, or begin the Presenters' Challenge.

Remember that children should remove their name badges before leaving the group area.

Debrief and clear-up (10 mins)

Before you start to clear up, pause together as a team and take time to reflect and evaluate the day. What worked well? Did anything not work well? What signs have you seen of God at work? How has God answered your prayers from earlier? Pray again for the children and the conversations they will be having at home.

Clear up and do any necessary preparation for tomorrow.

DAY 2

WHAT DID JESUS DO AND SAY?

 **BIBLE PASSAGE**
Luke 5:1–32

 **DIARY OF A DISCIPLE: LUKE'S STORY**
pages **70** to **88**

BEFORE YOUR CLUB BEGINS

Team preparation

Prepare the room first and then, 20 minutes before children will arrive, gather the team to prepare themselves.

Talk about the overall theme for the day, remind team members of the narratives being used, and read some of the verses together. Answer for yourselves the Question of the Day and the further questions. (Remind everyone that what they say in this time may not be appropriate to repeat to the children.) Pray for one another and for the club, the children and God's work in everyone.

Registration

Check in those who came yesterday, give parents and carers collection slips and provide name labels for the children.

Have registration forms available to register new children (remember that no child should attend the club without permission from their parent or carer).

When registration ends, take the registers to each Group Leader, so that they have them in case of fire or other emergency.

YOU WILL NEED

Items from the **Every Day** list on page 15 plus:

Small group welcome
- [ ] lengths of lining paper or sheets of flip chart paper

Setting the scene
- [ ] scarves
- [ ] hats
- [ ] rugby/football team or badged school shirts for the Presenters
- [ ] other items that show allegiance to different teams displayed around the upfront area
- [ ] music for 'Mastermind' and a means of playing it (optional)

Exploring the story

 Word Zone
- [ ] *Diary of a Disciple: Luke's Story* open at pages 70–88
- [ ] *The Lion Storyteller Bible* open at pages 70–73 ('Jesus' Special Friends' and 'Down Through the Roof')
- [ ] Good News Bible or International Children's Bible open at Luke 5

 Colour Zone
- [ ] building blocks and people minifigures
- [ ] soft netting
- [ ] pipe cleaners

 **Quiet Zone**
- [ ] *Diary of a Disciple: Luke's Story* open at pages 70–88
- [ ] *The Lion Storyteller Bible* open at pages 70–73 ('Jesus' Special Friends' and 'Down Through the Roof')
- [ ] Good News Bible or International Children's Bible open at Luke 5

 **Listening Zone**
- [ ] tablets ready to play Guardians of Ancora: Jesus and the fishermen
- [ ] MP3 players with *Diary of a Disciple: Luke's Story* audiobook chapter 5

Talk and make
- [ ] standard, top-opening envelopes
- [ ] artwork for the paralysed man from page 47
- [ ] yarn

YOUR OUTLINE FOR

DAY 2 What did Jesus do and say?

Small-group time
15 minutes in small groups

Small-group welcome (15 mins)

You will need:
- ☐ lengths of lining paper or sheets of flip chart paper

Welcome the children and talk briefly about any teams they support (sporting or otherwise), and the colours those teams use in their kit or logo. Together, create one poster that represents all the teams your group supports. Be as creative as you want to about the layout: make one large emblem or have strips of colour like scarves. Encourage the children to come up with ideas. You may find that some children struggle to think of a 'team' they support; if this is the case, encourage them to imagine what a team logo might look like for a team of their own and then add this to the poster. Keep the poster with you as you move into 'Setting the scene'.

Together time
45 minutes all together

Setting the scene (20 mins)

You will need:
- ☐ scarves
- ☐ hats
- ☐ rugby/football team or badged school shirts for the Presenters
- ☐ other items that show allegiance to different teams displayed around the upfront area
- ☐ music for 'Mastermind' and a means of playing it (optional)

The Presenters should be wearing rugby or football shirts, scarves, hats etc – as many things as possible that show allegiance to a team, club or school. Their chairs should be angled at 45 degrees, so that they can easily look at one another and at the audience.

The Presenters welcome the children and say how pleased they are to see everyone. They should briefly remind the children of any important information, rules or health and safety matters. If they have received pictures or diary entries from yesterday's challenge, they could show one or two and explain that all of these will be displayed for everyone to see.

Presenter 1 asks Presenter 2 what they are wearing, and why. Their reply goes into lots of detail about the team/club/school. Presenter 1 sits in their chair and pretends to fall asleep as if bored, only waking when Presenter 2 shakes Presenter 1 by the arm and asks, 'Why do you support [name the team of Presenter 1's clothing]?' Presenter 1 replies 'Because I think I look good in [the colour of their team].'

Presenter 2 points out that you don't support a team just because you look good in their colour. To prove their argument, they ask several children which team they support, and why. (Presenters need to avoid making derogatory comments about teams, and to stop the children from doing that too.)

Presenter 1 wants Presenter 2 to prove that they know lots about their team, so says they will play Mastermind (they should briefly explain what the quiz is, for the benefit of any children who don't know, including that if a question is being asked when the buzzer goes for the end of time, the question master says, 'I've started, so I'll finish!').

Begin the quiz by playing or singing the music for this, if possible. Presenter 1 should have some questions ready to ask, but also invites the children to ask some of their own. (You will therefore need to be flexible with the time!) As well as questions about the club, Presenter 1 could include the following:

- Why do you follow this team?
- What do you like or admire about them?
- How long have you followed them?
- Name three things that show you follow the club (eg watch matches, read their magazine, check the results).
- What's the best thing about following this team?

While the last question is being asked, have someone make a sound like the buzzer signalling the end of the contestant's time, so that Presenter 1 can say, 'I've started, so I'll finish!' and end the question, allowing Presenter 2 to complete their answer.

The Presenters invite each group, in turn, to show their banner or poster representing the teams they support. They then ask some of the leaders which team they support, the last of whom should say: 'I support Team Jesus.'

The Presenters appear confused but interested in what Team Jesus is all about, and call the leader on to the stage area and repeat the Mastermind-style questions, with this leader sitting in one of the chairs:

- Why do you follow Jesus?
- What do you like or admire about him?
- How long have you followed Jesus?
- Name three things you do that show you follow Jesus (eg read about him in the Bible, talk to him, meet up with other people who follow him).
- What's the best thing about following Jesus?

The Presenters then invite the children to ask questions about following Jesus. (Depending on the children at your club, you may need to 'plant' a few initial questions with Group Helpers.) When questions seem to be drying up (or if the children's questions go off topic), a Presenter asks one final question, during which someone makes the buzzer sound for the end of the time, so that 'I've started, so I'll finish!' can be said again.

The Presenters thank the children for their questions and the leader for their answers and explain that lots of others in the room also follow Jesus; they invite other followers to put up their hands (if there are very few at your club who don't follow Jesus, they should instead talk about how many followers of Jesus there are around the world).

The Presenters point out that Jesus must be really amazing if all these people follow him, so it's time to find out more in today's story!

Sharing the story (15 mins)

There are four different ways of sharing the story each day. Feel free to mix and match these approaches or use the same format every day, if this will work better in your context.

It's important the children know that the stories they hear or watch come from the Bible. Show a copy of *Diary of a Disciple: Luke's Story* and explain that it is based on the book in the Bible written by a man called Luke. Say that your story is a re-telling Luke's book in the Bible and it really happened: this isn't a made-up story.

Option 1: Drama
A drama script re-telling today's story, based on the text from *Diary of a Disciple: Luke's Story* is available to download from su.org.uk/DiaryHolidayClub.

Option 2: Audio story
An MP3 audio file telling today's story (from the *Diary of a Disciple: Luke's Story* audiobook) is available to download from su.org.uk/DiaryHolidayClub.

Option 3: Animation
An MP4 video animation telling today's story is available to download from su.org.uk/DiaryHolidayClub.

Option 4: Reading aloud
Depending on your context, you may wish to have a storyteller each day who sits down and reads aloud the story from *Diary of a*

Disciple: Luke's Story pages 70 to 88. This should be a volunteer from your team who is confident in reading aloud and will help the story to come alive as they read. You may wish to have the same storyteller for every session of your club, or you may prefer to have a different storyteller each day.

When the story has finished the Presenters should thank anyone who has helped to tell it, and comment about how amazing Jesus is: no wonder people follow him!

Everybody active! (10 mins)

Lead an energetic exercise or dance steps session to some lively music with a good strong beat.

Zone time
30 minutes in Zones

Exploring the story (30 mins)

The Presenters should explain that everyone is going to explore the story, and there lots of different ways of doing this. They should briefly remind everyone of the different Zones (using the explanations from page 9) and say there is an important question to think about:

HOW DOES WHAT JESUS DID AND SAID MAKE YOU FEEL?

Further questions for the children to explore are:

- What part might God want you to play?
- Why does God want you to be part of his plan?
- What would you like to say to God?

The Presenters should tell the children how long they have got to explore the story and say they can go to whichever Zone they like, and they can either stay there all the time or visit some other Zones too. (It's very important the children are allowed to choose the Zone or Zones that works best for them.) Any child who is unsure of what to do or where to go should come to the front or ask their Group Leader for help. They then send the children off to Zones.

In the various Zones, invite the children to explore the questions which are printed out and displayed; Zone Guides should encourage the children to keep thinking about them. You will also be serving refreshments during this time; remember to keep a check on who has had them.

 Word Zone

You will need:
- *Diary of a Disciple: Luke's Story* open at pages 70–88
- *The Lion Storyteller Bible* open at pages 70–73 ('Jesus' Special Friends' and 'Down Through the Roof')
- Good News Bible or International Children's Bible open at Luke 5

Encourage the children to explore the different versions of the stories and to write down anything that strikes them as they think about the Question of the Day and other questions.

 Colour Zone

You will need
- building blocks and people minifigures
- soft netting
- chenille wires

Encourage the children to interact with the different stories by building, recreating or drawing them.

 **Busy Zone**

Stuck in the Mud

Play the game in a hall or safe outdoor space.

Choose one or two children to be the chasers, and tell the rest of the children they are the evaders, and their aim it to evade the chasers. Say that, if a chaser catches (taps on the shoulder) an evader, that person is stuck in the mud and unable to move until another evader taps them on the shoulder.

Explain that the chasers win when all the evaders are stuck, and challenge the evaders to keep the game going as long as possible by freeing stuck teammates.

Play for a while and then talk together:

- What's the best way to win as the chaser?
- What is the best way to win as the evaders?

Encourage any who have struggled with the game to remember these tips and play the game again. Then, while the children have refreshments, discuss these questions:

- What does it feel like to be stuck in the mud, with no one coming to help you?
- What does it feel like to be freed?
- Do you think things ever happen to us that make us feel as though we're stuck in mud, even if we're not literally there? Can you think of anything that has ever made you feel like that? (One of the leaders may be able to tell them a short, appropriate story when something they did or something that was happening in their life made them feel as though they were stuck in mud.)
- Question of the Day: How does what did Jesus did and said make you feel?

Conclude with the following words, or similar:

I wonder how the paralysed man felt. Maybe he felt a bit stuck in the mud. Thankfully, he had friends who wanted to help, but they could only do so much. In the end, it was only Jesus who could help and free him. I wonder what he felt after he was freed.

End the session with another round of Stuck in the Mud.

 **Quiet Zone**

You will need:
- ☐ *Diary of a Disciple: Luke's Story* open at pages 70–88
- ☐ *The Lion Storyteller Bible* open at pages 70–73 ('Jesus' Special Friends' and 'Down Through the Roof')
- ☐ Good News Bible or International Children's Bible open at Luke 5

Around the walls of the space you are using, display the Question of the Day and some of the pictures from the Day's image collection, and have the books available for any child who wants to read the passage again. Allow children to sit here quietly or to explore the story again.

 Chat Zone

Chat with children about the story and questions. You may need to ask questions to get the conversation started, such as 'Which part of the story did you like best? Why?' But some children will just want to chat about anything and everything! Allow them to do so, as this builds strong relationships, but then focus the chat a little by asking them one or two questions about the story, including the Question of the Day. They need to know that you are genuinely interested in them and their lives, not just their response to the story.

You should also explain to the children that there may be things in their lives that they find difficult, or sad, and that they would like to talk about. If so, they can just say 'I want some help' and you or another leader will know they want to talk about something important, and will help them (in line with your organisation's safeguarding policy).

 Listening Zone

You will need:
- ☐ tablets ready to play Guardians of Ancora: Jesus and the fishermen
- ☐ MP3 players with *Diary of a Disciple: Luke's Story* audiobook chapter 5

Invite children to play the quest on the tablets. Remind them that they can also do

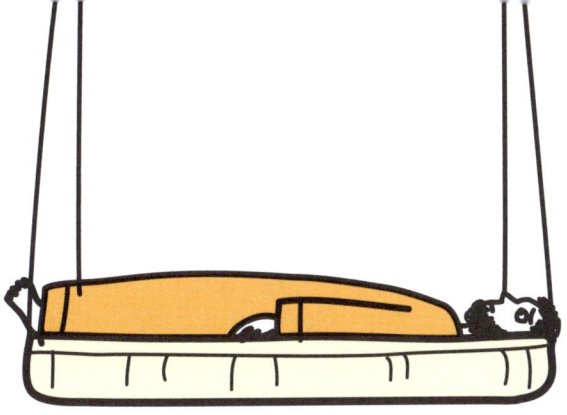

a quiz on the story once it's completed (you will need to show them where to find this).

They can also listen to the audio story, if available, on devices.

At the end of 'Exploring the story', send the children back to their small groups. You may want to play some music to signify that the time is ending – perhaps start it quietly two to three minutes before the end of the time and turn the volume up slowly. This way Zone Guides will know to start winding up the activities and sending children back to their small groups, without having to watch the time!

Small-group time
45 minutes in small groups

Talk and make (30 mins)

You will need:
- ☐ standard, top-opening envelopes
- ☐ the paralysed man artwork from page 47
- ☐ yarn

Invite the children to tell you what they did and what they discovered in the Explore Zones that helped them to answer the Question of the Day: 'How does what did Jesus did and said make you feel?'

Encourage the children to listen to one another. Write down what each child says, even if you disagree with it, using the whiteboard (or clipboard and paper). Add in your own answer, perhaps doing this first to set the example. Be ready to gently correct anything that is wildly inaccurate (see pages 18 and 19 for more about how and why).

Move on to the day's making activity while keeping the discussion going. Explain that what they make will help them to remember today's story, and encourage them to keep on thinking about the Question of the Day. Discuss the extra questions for the day, though you don't need to write down all the answers to these. (Don't make this conversation a formal question and answer session; rather, aim to keep the atmosphere as relaxed as possible.)

Story envelopes

1. In advance, cut a large window in the front of each envelope and a slit in the middle of the top flap. Make sure you have reproduced the paralysed man artwork at a suitable size for the envelope you are using – he needs to be just shorter than the size of the window.

2. Give each child an envelope and invite them to draw windows and a door on the back.

DIARY DAYS

3 Show them how to turn the envelope round and draw people on the inside, so that they are visible through the cut window. Encourage them to make one of the people very obviously Jesus, and to fill the rest of the space with other people.

4 Give each child a copy of the paralysed man artwork from page 47 and invite them to colour it in and cut it out.

5 Help them to wrap one piece of wool around his shoulders and one round his lower legs, but don't tie them.

6 Demonstrate how to use the model to tell the story: Start with the flap up and explain that houses in our country usually have a sloping roof. Then fold it down and explain that houses in the country where the story happened had a flat roof. Turn the envelope round and tell the story, showing the house full of people. At the appropriate moment, lower the man through the slit in the roof, in front of Jesus (you may need help to open the slit and lower the figure). When Jesus finally tells him to get up, remove the wool from around his legs and stand him up in the 'house', and then remove the wool from his shoulders.

7 Encourage the children to practise telling the story so they can tell it to their families later.

Journal time (15 mins)

Clear away the craft materials. Give each child a copy of the *Day Book* (5 to 8s) or *Jotter* (8 to 11s). Invite them to spend some time completing pages 10 to 14 (*Day Book*) or pages 12 to 19 (*Jotter*) as they reflect on all that they have discovered today.

When your club ends
30 minutes

Children are collected (10 mins)

Remind the children of the Presenters' Challenge: to draw a picture that illustrates one of the stories from that day, or to re-tell one of the stories in the style of Luke's diary (but not just copying what's in the book!), or to make a diary entry about their own day in the style of Luke's diary.

Say that the challenge is optional, it's not homework, but if any child wants to do it they should bring their entry, with their name on, tomorrow, and give it to their Group Leader.

As you wait for parents and carers to collect their children, invite them to complete some of the extra pages in their *Day Book* or *Jotter*. Alternatively, they could work on further decoration of your group home area, or begin the Presenters' Challenge.

Remember that children should remove their name badges before leaving the group area.

Debrief and clearing up (10 mins)

Before you start to clear up, meet together as a team to reflect and evaluate the day. What did the children particularly enjoy? Were there any problems? Try to resolve any that arise. What signs have you seen of God at work? How has God answered your prayers from earlier? Pray again for the children and the conversations they will be having at home.

Clear up and prepare for tomorrow; display any entries for the Presenters' Challenge. If tomorrow is the last day of your club, remember to get ready any flyers advertising clubs or other events at the church for handing out.

2 WHAT DID JESUS DO AND SAY?

DAY 2 What did Jesus do and say?

PHOTOCOPIABLE PAGE

47

DIARY DAYS

DAY 3
WHAT HAPPENED TO JESUS?

BIBLE PASSAGE
Luke 22:1–24, 39–54, 63–71; 23:1–5, 13–46, 50–56; 24:1–31

DIARY OF A DISCIPLE: LUKE'S STORY
chapters **22**, **23** and **24**

BEFORE YOUR CLUB BEGINS

Team preparation

Have the room and different areas ready 20 minutes before the children will arrive, and then gather as a team to prepare yourselves. Remind team members of the overall theme for the day and the narratives being used. Read one or two of them. Answer for yourselves the Question of the Day and the further questions. (Remind everyone that what they say in this time may not be appropriate to repeat to the children.) Pray for one another and for the club, for God's work in the children and especially for the Holy Spirit to help each one to recognise who Jesus is.

Registration

You will need:
☐ any flyers or invitations to future events

Welcome and register the children as usual. Even though this is the final day of your club, you may have new children attending – be ready for them.

If you plan to invite the children to any clubs or activities as a follow-on to your holiday club, it would be good to have flyers ready with details of these. Put some on the registration desk; each group should have them too, ready to give one to each child as they leave at the end of the session. When registration ends, take the registers to each Group Leader so they have them in case of fire or other emergencies.

YOU WILL NEED

Items from the **Every Day** list on page 15 plus:

Registration
- [ ] any flyers or invitations to future events

Setting the scene
- [ ] a washing line with the word 'Goodbye!' pegged on it as individual letters
- [ ] a set of table tennis balls with group names or numbers on them, held in a see-through container
- [ ] a vacuum cleaner with a nozzle smaller than the diameter of a table tennis ball (and a power supply for this)
- [ ] a small whiteboard per group and whiteboard marker, or pieces of card and a marker pen
- [ ] sheets of paper or card with numbers on one side and the answers to the quiz questions on the other
- [ ] a display board

Exploring the story

 Word Zone
- [ ] *Diary of a Disciple: Luke's Story* open at pages 310–314, 317–323, 325–332, 335–345
- [ ] *The Lion Storyteller Bible* open at pages 106–109 ('A Dreadful Day and A Happy Day')
- [ ] Good News Bible or International Children's Bible open at Luke 22–24

 Colour Zone
- [ ] materials for junk modelling (such as boxes, tubs, packets)
- [ ] twigs
- [ ] string

 Busy Zone
- [ ] an equal number of cones and soft balls that will balance on top of them (10 or more depending on the size of your group)
- [ ] 6 hoops

 **Quiet Zone**
- [ ] *Diary of a Disciple: Luke's Story* open at pages 310–314, 317–323, 325–332, 335–345
- [ ] *The Lion Storyteller Bible* open at pages 106–109 ('A Dreadful Day and A Happy Day')
- [ ] Good News Bible or International Children's Bible open at Luke 22–24

 Listening Zone
- [ ] tablets ready to play Guardians of Ancora: The Way to the Cross
- [ ] MP3 players with *Diary of a Disciple: Luke's Story* audiobook chapters 22, 23, 24

Talk and make
- [ ] copies of the cube artwork from page 58
- [ ] double-sided sticky tape or PVA glue and spreaders

Children are collected
- [ ] any information flyers that you are giving out

DAY 3 What happened to Jesus?

YOUR OUTLINE FOR DAY 3

Small-group time
15 minutes in small groups

Small group welcome (15 mins)

Welcome the children and chat about what they did yesterday after the club. Being genuinely interested in the children's lives (but not too nosey!) helps to build relationships of trust and openness. But also talk together about what everyone will do after the club: immediately (go home, have lunch etc), later today… next week… when school starts again etc. When you have listened to the children's plans, tell them about any plans the church has to run other events that they might like to come to.

Together time
45 minutes all together

Setting the scene (20 mins)

You will need: a washing line with the word 'Goodbye!' pegged on it as individual letters; a set of table tennis balls with group names or numbers on them, held in a see-through container; a vacuum cleaner with a nozzle smaller than the diameter of a table tennis ball (and a power supply for this); a small whiteboard per group and whiteboard marker, or pieces of card and a marker pen; sheets of paper or card with numbers on one side and the answers to the quiz questions on the other; a display board

Prepare the quiz by writing the numbers 1 to 9 (more if you have more than nine groups or want to ask more than nine questions) on one side of the sheets of paper or card. Write the answer to one of the quiz questions on the back of each numbered sheet, in a random order. (Don't put the answer to the first question on the back of number 1, etc!) Attach your numbered sheets to the display board with the number showing and the answer hidden (they need to be removed and replaced easily).

Set the 'Goodbye' washing line and the quiz up in your upfront area, ready for the Presenters and children to arrive.

The Presenters come running on and shout hello, getting the children cheering. They milk this somewhat, with separate hellos to the girls, the boys and the leaders, etc. One asks the other why so many hellos and is told it's to counteract the bunting that says goodbye, and they don't want the children to leave yet. There's some discussion about why there's a goodbye banner up, and speculation about who might be leaving, until they realise that today is the end of the holiday club. (*Sighs all round.*) That means that EVERYONE is leaving! (*More sighs all round.*) But it also means that everyone can come back next time there's another event like this! (*Cheers all round.*) Show one or two diary or picture entries from the Challenge, reminders of the great time everyone has had, and remind the children to look at all of them on display.

Presenter 1 says that on their family holidays, at the end of the time away, they discuss what they've done and decide what their favourite part of the holiday has been. They say they think it would be a great idea to do this for the *Diary of a Disciple* holiday club too! So, to help everyone decide, there's going to be a competition.

Presenter 2 is really excited about this and organises the children to huddle round their Group Leaders, because everyone is playing this in their groups. They challenge every group to decide what has been their favourite thing during the week, and then to make up a quick mime – no more than 30 seconds long – to explain it to other groups. They give the groups 2 minutes to decide what they will do. (It doesn't matter if two teams choose the same thing, as long as they don't copy each other's mimes.)

The Presenters explain they will use the Random Selector to choose which group comes out to mime each time. They turn on the vacuum, hold it above the container of table tennis balls and suck up one. They call that group out to the front to perform their mime. They challenge everyone else to watch carefully, decide in their group what the activity was and write it on their whiteboard or card. After 15 seconds, the Presenters invite all groups to hold up their guess: the team that mimed scores one point for every group that guesses correctly. Each team that guesses correctly also scores 1 point (Group Leaders will need to keep a count of scores).

The Presenters use the Random Selector to choose the next team, and so on, until all have had a go. They check the groups' scores and invite the winners to take a bow.

Next the Presenters announce a quiz on the stories from the week, and say this will be done in groups.

They show the board with numbers and explain that the quiz answers are muddled up on the backs of the numbers. Nobody knows which answer is behind which number, so it will all be guesswork – to begin with.

The Presenters return the balls to the container and use the Random Selector to choose a group to answer each question in turn. They read out a question and challenge the group to choose a number from the board. They turn that numbered sheet over and read out the answer on the back. If the answer is correct, that team gets a point and the Presenters place the answer on the board facing outwards. If incorrect, they replace it with the number side out again. (They should not allow another group to have a guess.) Of course, there may be times when the correct number is chosen by chance, but in time it will also be about children remembering which answer is where. Sometimes they may be fortunate because the previous group has just turned up their answer!

To make sure each group gets a turn, once a group answered, the Presenters should put that group's ball to one side until all balls have been used. If there are still questions to be answered, they should return all balls to the container and start again, keeping going through the questions until all have been answered. It will get easier and quicker as they get further through the questions!

Possible questions and their answers are listed below. Check that the children were told all these stories, and create some alternative questions if not. The questions below are based on the three main Days; if your club includes Additional Days, you might want to include something from those stories.

- The angel told Mary that her baby would be the Son of…? (God)
- To where did Mary and Joseph have to travel? (Bethlehem)
- Who told the shepherds about the baby? (An angel)
- What did Simeon say Jesus would be? (A light)
- What did Jesus tell Simon and his friends to do? (Follow him)
- What was wrong with the skin of the man Jesus healed? (Lumpy and bumpy)
- How many friends carried the man to Jesus on a mat? (Four)
- Why didn't the Pharisees think Jesus could forgive sins? (Only God can)
- What was the name of the tax collector who followed Jesus? (Levi)

Finally, the Presenters should encourage the groups to huddle again for 30 seconds to decide which was their favourite story, and then ask each group in turn for their answer.

The Presenters conclude by saying that all the stories at the club have shown us how amazing Jesus is! (They could summarise what he did and said.) They say it seems to make sense that everyone would've loved Jesus and wanted him to help them, but they've heard that some people really didn't. They look confused and say they think everyone should find out what happened.

Sharing the story (15 mins)

There are four different ways of sharing the story each day. Feel free to mix and match these approaches or use the same format every day, if this will work better in your context.

It's important that the children know that the stories they hear or watch come from the Bible. Show a copy of *Diary of a Disciple: Luke's Story* and explain that it is based on the book in the Bible written by a man called Luke. Say that your story is a re-telling of Luke's book in the Bible and it really happened: this isn't a made-up story.

Option 1: Drama
A drama script re-telling today's story, based on the text from *Diary of a Disciple: Luke's Story* is available to download from **su.org.uk/DiaryHolidayClub**.

Option 2: Audio story
An MP3 audio file telling today's story (from the *Diary of a Disciple: Luke's Story* audiobook) is available to download from **su.org.uk/DiaryHolidayClub**.

Option 3: Animation
An MP4 video animation telling today's story is available to download from **su.org.uk/DiaryHolidayClub**.

Option 4: Reading aloud
Depending on your context, you may wish to have a storyteller each day who sits down and reads aloud the story from *Diary of a Disciple: Luke's Story* chapters 22 to 24. This should be a volunteer from your team who is confident in reading aloud and will help the story to come alive as they read. You may wish to have the same storyteller for every session of your club, or you may prefer to have a different storyteller each day.

Today's story: pages 302–307 (ending with 'about who was the best'); pages 310–314 (starting with 'Jesus was heading back' and ending with 'They led Jesus away'); pages 317–323 (starting with '…the guards who were keeping an eye' and ending with 'disturbing everything!'); pages 325–332 (starting with 'Pilate pulled everyone' and ending with 'And then he died.'); pages 335–345 (starting with 'Joseph took Jesus' body' and ending with 'Jesus had vanished').

When the story has finished the Presenters should thank anyone who has helped to tell it, and comment about how incredible it was that, despite what Jesus had done to help and heal so many people, some hated him enough to have him killed. But it's even more incredible that God brought him back to life!

Everybody active! (10 mins)

Lead simple exercises or dance moves so that the children (and leaders!) burn off some energy.

The Presenters bring 'Together time' to a close a little earlier than usual, and tell children about any clubs or activities the church runs to which they might like to come. They keep this short and have a flyer about them to give to each child at the end of the club. The Presenters remind the children they can continue the Presenters' Challenge and write or draw something that sums up the whole week, but this time display it at home, not at the club.

Zone time
30 minutes in Zones

Exploring the story (30 mins)

The Presenters should explain that everyone is going to explore the story, and there lots of different ways of doing this. They should briefly describe the different Zones (using the explanations from page 9) and say there is an important question to think about:

HOW DO YOU FEEL ABOUT WHAT HAPPENED TO JESUS?

There are also some other questions:

- What surprised you in this story?
- Do you think that Jesus is alive today? Why?
- What difference might knowing this story make to your life?
- Now that you have heard this story – the story of Easter – who do you think Jesus is?

The Presenters should tell the children how long they have got to explore the story and say they can go to whichever Zone they like, and they can either stay there all the time or visit some other Zones too. (It's very important the children are allowed to choose the Zone or Zones that works best for them.) Any child who is unsure of what to do or where to go should come to the front or ask their Group Leader for help. They then send the children off to Zones.

In the various Zones, invite the children to explore the questions which are printed out and displayed; Zone Guides should encourage the children to keep thinking about them. You will also be serving refreshments during this time; remember to keep a check on who has had them.

Word Zone

You will need:
- ☐ *Diary of a Disciple: Luke's Story* open at pages 310–314, 317–323, 325–332, 335–345
- ☐ *The Lion Storyteller Bible* open at pages 106–109 ('A Dreadful Day and A Happy Day')
- ☐ Good News Bible or International Children's Bible open at Luke 22–24

Encourage the children to explore the different versions of the stories and to write down anything that strikes them as they think about the questions of the day.

Colour Zone

You will need:
- ☐ materials for junk modelling (such as boxes, tubs, packets)
- ☐ twigs
- ☐ string

Encourage the children to interact with the different stories by building/re-creating/drawing them.

Busy Zone

You will need:
- ☐ an equal number of cones and soft balls that will balance on top of them (10 or more depending on the size of your group)
- ☐ 6 hoops

Underarm dodgeball

Use a line of cones to divide the hall in half, and place a soft ball on top of each cone. Place three hoops in each half of the hall in random spaces (see diagram on page 54).

Split the children into two teams and invite them to stand at opposite ends of the hall with their backs against the wall. If you have a large number of children, you could split them into smaller teams. (If you do, you will need to create an activity for teams to do off the pitch while not playing, such as having some simple wooden puzzles that

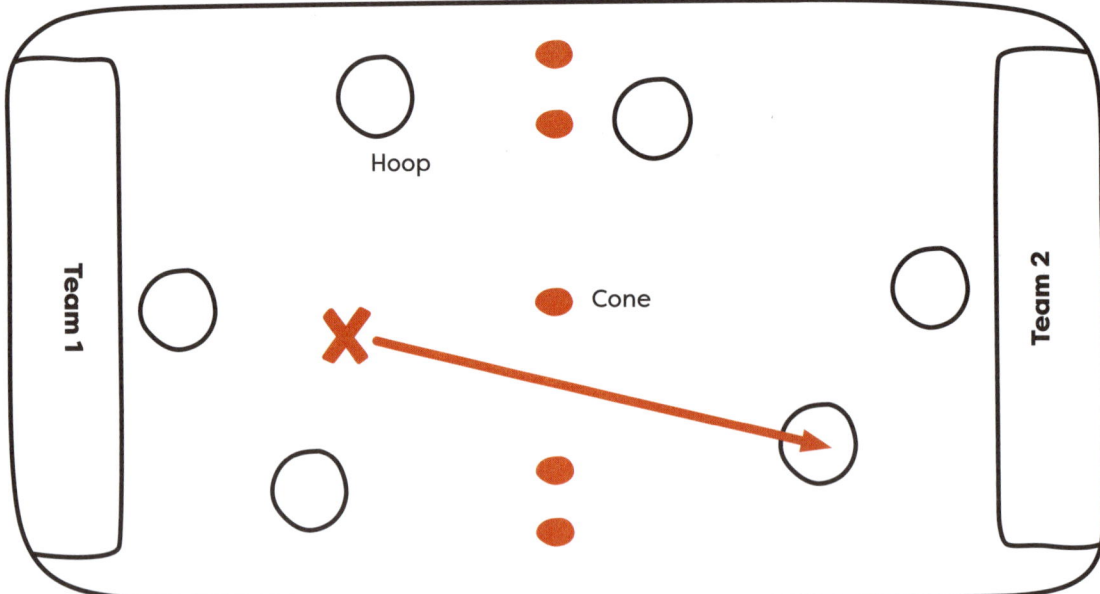

the children can try to solve. This is a risky time when bored children start to argue or get in trouble for messing with things! Keep the children active all the time.

Explain that the aim of the game is to try to capture three opposing team members by hitting each once with a soft ball, and to avoid being hit and therefore captured themselves. Say that when a team member has been hit by one of the opposing team's balls, they must go to stand in a hoop on the opposing team's side of the hall.

Run through the rest of the rules, as follows:

- When the game starts, the children should run to grab a soft ball from the top of a cone but MUST return to the rear part of their half of the room before they can throw it.
- Each child can only carry one ball.
- Soft balls must be thrown underarm, and below head height.
- If a child is holding a ball, they can use it to block an incoming ball. They cannot hit it away with their hands or catch it, they can only dodge away from it and then run after it to pick it up.
- Any child hit by an opposing team's ball is captured (see 'X' on diagram) and must go and stand in a hoop in the opposing team's half. But if they are hit on the head (as this isn't allowed), the person who threw the ball is captured instead!
- A captive can be freed if they catch a ball that is thrown to them by one of their own team members. Freed captives can now carry two soft balls (using one to block for protection and one to throw as a missile).
- A team wins when they manage to fill their three hoops, ie catch three opposing team members.

Begin the game.

Variation

Instead of standing in hoops, if a child is hit by a soft ball they must stop playing, go to the side line and perform ten star jumps and five squats before they come back into the game. The game ends when four or more children from one team are on the side lines at the same time.

When all teams have played, pause the game and talk together. You could have refreshments at this point.

- What were your tactics to win?
- What emotions did you feel during the game? (*Excitement, fear, other?*)
- What emotions do you think Jesus felt while he was being arrested and tried?
- Was it better to get people caught so they could come back and then hold two balls?
- Did anyone deliberately try to get hit so that they could come back stronger?
- Do you think that Jesus came back stronger?

- Question of the Day: How do you feel about what happened to Jesus?

After a break, change the teams around, giving you a chance to level up any discrepancies in skills, and play again.

 **Quiet Zone**

You will need:
- *Diary of a Disciple: Luke's Story* open at pages 310–314, 317–323, 325–332, 335–345
- *The Lion Storyteller Bible* open at pages 106–109 ('A Dreadful Day and A Happy Day')
- Good News Bible or International Children's Bible open at Luke 22–24

Allow the children to sit quietly and think about the stories. You might want to put some of the pictures from the image collection here to help children's thinking, along with Bibles.

 **Chat Zone**

Chat with children about the story and questions. You may need to ask questions to get the conversation started, such as 'Which part of the story did you like best? Why?' But some children will just want to chat about anything and everything! Allow them to do so, as this builds strong relationships, but then focus the chat a little by asking them one or two questions about the story, including the Question of the Day. They need to know that you are genuinely interested in them and their lives, not just their response to the story.

You should also explain to the children that there may be things in their lives that they find difficult, or sad, and that they would like to talk about. If so, they can just say 'I want some help' and you or another leader will know they want to talk about something important, and will help them (in line with your organisation's safeguarding policy).

Listening Zone

You will need:
- tablets ready to play Guardians of Ancora: The Way to the Cross
- MP3 players with *Diary of a Disciple: Luke's Story* audiobook chapters 22 to 24

Invite the children to play the quest on the tablets. Remind them that they can also do a quiz on the story once it's completed (you will need to show them where to find this). They can also listen to the audio story, if available, on devices.

At the end of 'Exploring the story', send the children back to their small groups. You may want to play some music to signify that the time is ending – perhaps start it quietly two to three minutes before the end of the time and turn the volume up slowly. This way Zone Guides will know to start winding up the activities and sending children back to their small groups, without having to watch the time!

Small-group time
45 minutes in small groups

Talk and make (30 mins)

You will need:
- copies of the cube artwork from page 58
- double-sided sticky tape or PVA glue and spreaders

Invite the children to tell you what they did and what they discovered in the Explore Zones that helped them to answer the Question of the Day: 'How do you feel about what happened to Jesus?'

Encourage the children to listen to one another. Write down what each child says, even if you disagree with it, using the whiteboard (or clipboard and paper). Add in your own answer, perhaps doing this first to set the example. Be ready to gently correct anything that is wildly inaccurate (see pages 18 and 19 for more about how and why).

Move on to the day's making activity while keeping the discussion going. Explain that what they make will help them to remember today's story, and to keep on thinking about the question. Discuss the extra questions for the day, though you don't need to write down all the answers to these. Group Leaders should not make this conversation a formal question and answer session; rather, they should aim to keep the atmosphere as relaxed as possible. Further questions for the children to explore today are: 'What surprised you in this story? Do you think that Jesus is alive today? Why? What difference might knowing this story make to your life? Now that you have heard this story – the story of Easter – who do you think Jesus is?'

Jesus cube

1 Give each child a copy of the cube artwork from page 58.
2 Challenge the children to find the different names for Jesus written on the cube. Explain that these are some of the things that have been said about Jesus. Invite the children to colour in the cube artwork and, as they work, to think about whether or not they think each name is a good way of describing Jesus. (Make it clear that there isn't a 'right' answer, you just want them to consider their own opinion.)

3 Demonstrate how to cut out the cube, crease carefully along the flaps and folds and fold into a cube shape.

4 Help the children to glue the flaps or stick with double-sided sticky tape to make their cube together.
5 Talk together about the different stories about Jesus they have heard during holiday club, and what they help us to understand about him.
6 You have asked the children a lot of questions through the week: in return, invite them to ask any questions of you or your Group Helpers.

3 WHAT HAPPENED TO JESUS?

Journal time (15 mins)

Clear away the craft materials. Give each child a copy of the *Day Book* (5 to 8s) or *Jotter* (8 to 11s). Invite them to spend some time completing pages 15 to 19 (*Day Book*) or pages 20 to 25 (*Jotter*) as they reflect on all that they have discovered today.

It would be good to lead the group in a short prayer thanking God for the things they have enjoyed or learned at the club. If you have not used the Additional Day 2 outline on prayer, you will need to explain that prayer is talking to God; that even though we can't see him, we can talk to him like we talk to our friends or families. Explain that when people pray together, they often say the word 'Amen' at the end: it means 'I agree'. Invite everyone to sit round in a circle; explain that you will start the prayer with 'Thank you God for these things we've enjoyed this week'. You will then go round the circle (show the direction) and anyone who wants to say even just one word or phrase can do so when it's their turn. If they don't want to say anything, that's fine – they can just shake their head and you will invite the next person to say something, if they want to. When you have gone round the whole circle, end the prayer with 'Amen'; those who want to can join in, if they agree with the prayer.

When your club ends
30 minutes

Children are collected (10 mins)

You will need:
☐ any information flyers that you are giving out

Make sure that each child takes home everything that is theirs: jumpers, coats, things they have made etc. Check that nothing that belongs to a child has been left in your group's box.

If the children want to take home some of the group's decoration, create a fair way to do this if there are more children than available pieces, rather than give things to the first child who asks.

As you say goodbye, thank the children for coming, and thank the parents for bringing them.

Parents often stand and talk to one another and to the leaders on the final day, so once everyone has their belongings ready, remind them of about any follow-on activities that your church is running and give everyone any information flyers. If any children are still waiting, encourage them to start the Presenters' Challenge and write about the whole week in the style of *Diary of a Disciple: Luke's Story*. Make sure they take this with them to complete at home.

Debrief and clearing up (10 mins)

Before you start to clear up, meet together as a team to reflect and evaluate today and, briefly, the club as a whole (though it would be good to meet together in a week or so to do this more thoroughly). How have you seen God at work in the children? In the team? Among parents? How has God answered your prayers for the week? Spend time thanking him for all he has done, and pray for the children and their families, and for God's ongoing work in them.

DAY 3 What happened to Jesus?

57

DIARY DAYS

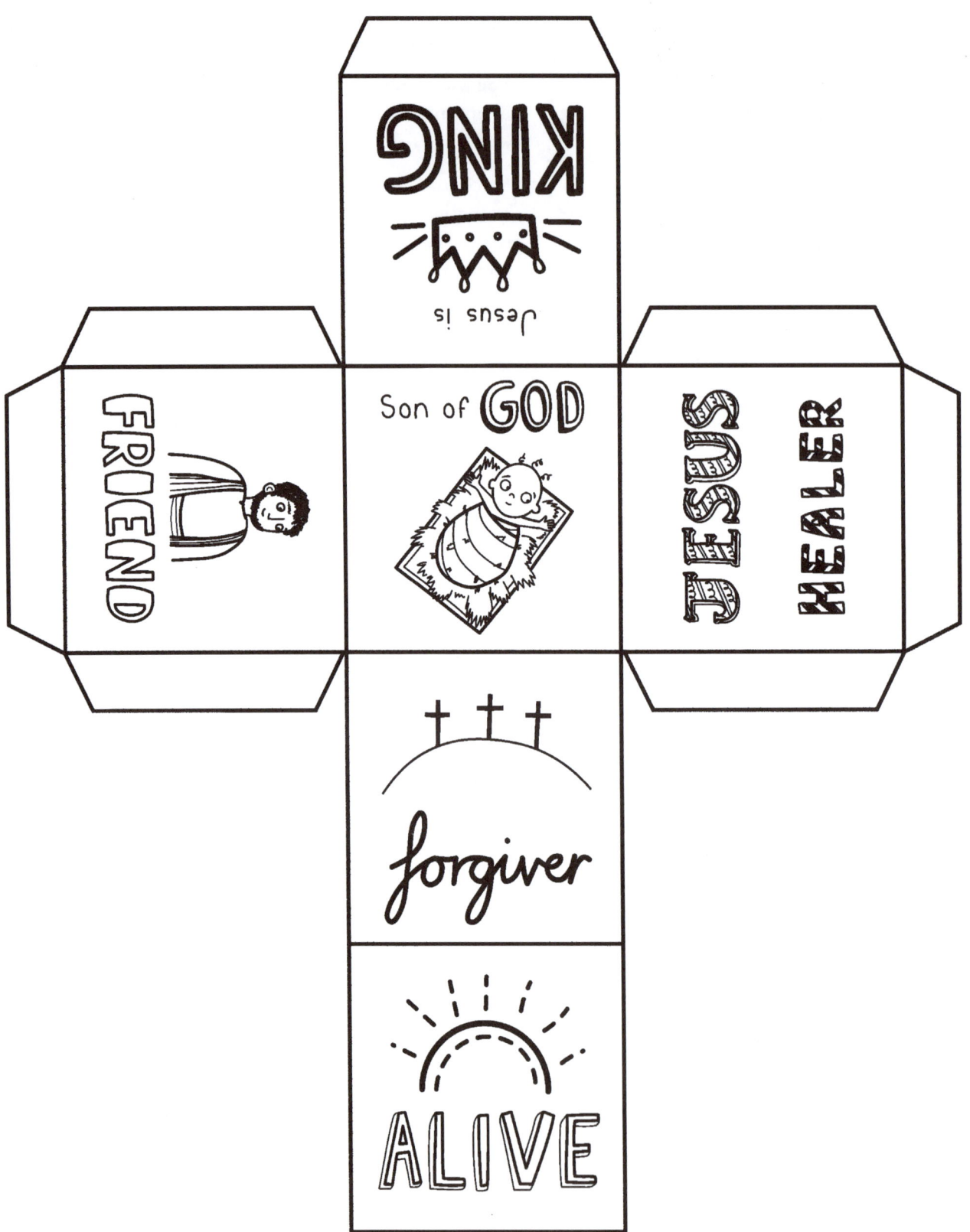

PHOTOCOPIABLE PAGE

FOLLOW-ON

FOLLOW-ON

FAITH JOURNEYS

Back to that important topic: 'What do you do to follow on from your holiday club?'

At the beginning of this resource book we thought about this from the perspective of the church, and activities you could plan that would maintain and build on your contact with the children (page 28). Now we're going to think about it from the children's perspective, taking into account the need to not just maintain contact, but to help the children move on in their journey towards or with God.

What each child needs to continue in their journey will vary. Some will need to explore Jesus and faith much more. The holiday club may have revealed a few pieces of a jigsaw, and they can see a bit of the picture, but there is a lot more to see before they are ready to decide who Jesus is, never mind consider whether they should follow him.

Others will have seen those same few pieces and worked out that Jesus is God's Son. They might need to explore a little more, but also be helped to think about the 'So what?' that follows knowing who Jesus is. They need to be encouraged to respond to Jesus. For the disciples in Luke's diary, the next step was to follow Jesus, but not every child will be ready for that level of response. For some, the response will simply be wanting to know more; some will want to hold on to the positives of the holiday club. Of course, some will want make a commitment to follow Jesus. It's important to allow the children to respond in their own way and at their own pace.

FOLLOW-ON

A regular club could help children to discover what following Jesus means and if it's the right thing for them. A regular club could also help them to grow as a disciple. Jesus' disciples went everywhere with him in order to do just that. Children can't do that, but by meeting regularly with others in a group, which takes things at the right speed and still makes no assumptions about what they know or believe, they can grow in their faith and belief. They could join a church group that already exists, but might find it difficult and drop out because so much is new to them. A new group, set up with the aim of helping them to discover more, would be better.

To find out more about how you can walk alongside children as they explore who Jesus is, consider their response to him and hopefully go on to grow in a vibrant, personal faith in Jesus, contact your local Scripture Union Mission Enabler. Go to our website **www.scriptureunion.org.uk**.

NOTES